PREDICTABLY BROKEN

PREDICTABLY BROKEN

Straight Talk on Failures in Biopharma Operations
and How to Fix Them

Oscar A. González

SYNAPSE BREW
PUBLISHING

Synapse Brew Publishing
synapsebrewpublishing.com

ISBN: 979-8-9934754-0-0 (paperback)
ISBN: 979-8-9934754-1-7 (ebook)
ISBN: 979-8-9934754-2-4 (hardcover)

Printed in Boston, MA

Library of Congress Control Number: 2025923870

Ordering Information:
Special discounts are available on quantity purchases by corporations, associations, and others. For details, visit synapsebrewpublishing.com.

Publisher's Cataloging-in-Publication Data
Names: Gonzalez, Oscar A., 1985– , author.
Title: predictably broken : straight talk on failures in biopharma operations and how to fix them / Oscar A. Gonzalez.
Description: Boston, MA : Synapse Brew Publishing, 2026 | Summary: A practical guide addressing operational inefficiencies in biopharma companies. Drawing on real-world experience, the author presents the Biopharma Nexus Model to improve research, portfolio, business operations, governance, and data systems in complex, regulated environments.
Identifiers: ISBN 979-8-9934754-2-4 (hardback) | ISBN 979-8-9934754-0-0 (pbk) | ISBN 979-8-9934754-1-7 (ebook) | LCCN 2025923870
Subjects: LCSH: Biotechnology industries—Management. | Pharmaceutical industry—Management. | Industrial management—Health aspects. | Organizational effectiveness. | Business planning. | BISAC: BUSINESS & ECONOMICS / Industries / Pharmaceutical & Biotechnology | BUSINESS & ECONOMICS / Management / General | BUSINESS & ECONOMICS / Strategic Planning
Classification: LCC HD9999.B44 G66 2026 (print) | DDC 338.476151—dc23

Dedication

*To the former version of me who thought success was a linear path—
and kept walking his own path anyway.*

TABLE OF CONTENTS

PROLOGUE

I DIDN'T SET out to create a framework. When it finally did come to me, I wasn't even sure what to call it. Or what it meant. My attempts to build a successful career steered me in directions I could not have foreseen. It also put me into situations or meetings where I questioned, "Am I supposed to be here?" The mere concept of efficiency and operational exposure wasn't even something that came to me until much later in life.

What I can say is that I have always loved science, but science didn't always love me back. Establishing a career in the life sciences was a dream, of which I had a very narrow perspective in my high school years. Even in the early days, I found myself marveled by Hollywood's interpretation of the medical field. You know, those hospital dramas where the team pulls the patient through a difficult time. The show *House* was a staple for my evening lineup. A medical drama that follows a diagnostician with a unique approach and set of skills, who nearly always came out on top, not without some wild drama. It gave me perspective on researching problems, looking outside the box, discussing concerns with colleagues, and finding the right solutions.

At a time when high schoolers are taught to plan their future, go to college, and then start a career, I was more focused on our upcoming varsity baseball game—for which I got to leave class early. From an education perspective, I was never really challenged until I went to college.

With a dream of becoming a trauma surgeon, I was humbled after two years at a four-year college. That dream became a distant finish line, with just two years to make my move to becoming a medical school contender. I never did.

A tough pill to swallow. I was so focused on achieving a goal, I never really knew what it took to get there. Other than academic struggles, I did not face adversity. Growing up, I was the "smart one." My father was an engineer for NASA for 40 years. This path was in my blood. Right?

I was not where I set out to be. Goals were just dreams because the work I did was not enough. Things just did not stick for me in the lecture hall. I was more of a hands-on learner. I needed to be in the thick of it to really gain insights and to learn. Maybe that realization is where my work all started.

It was toward the end of my bachelor's degree that I shifted my attention to research. On the recommendation of my physics professor, an engineer by trade, I continued on, enrolling in a new bachelor's program in biomedical engineering. The unfortunate part was recognizing that courses past Calculus 2 were simply too abstract for me to comprehend. I had to make a shift, again.

After working in retail and restaurants for a few years, I found my way back to the lab and started at the ground level. My engineering internship eventually got me in front of a principal investigator (PI) at a prestigious regenerative medicine laboratory in North Carolina. I had a new goal, to become a PhD so that I could do the research that drove my interests: oncology. Those years working in academic research gave me foundational knowledge of laboratory work- planning, SOPs, lab notebooks, documentation, funding, and regulations—all critical features of well-organized science. I recognized that my opportunities were launching pads to the next step toward earning a PhD.

I was once asked, "With so much money going into [cancer] research, why is there no cure?" A naive question, sure, but the essence of it stuck with me. Why is this industry incredibly expensive? And what is our role in it? My continued work in academia was the experience I needed to see something more critical than becoming a PhD—fixing a broken system.

That insight developed a new belief within me. I did not have to be the best scientist in the room to play my role in curing diseases. I could be an enabler through building connections, testing my own limitations for improvement, becoming a connector of people, data, strategies, and theories. The more I could continue to learn and advance my reasoning, the more valuable I would become to the people around me. My efforts stopped becoming about my career and became more about the impact I could have on those around me.

What I set out to do since that moment, and what I've continued to do, is to make work easier, smoother, and clearer—more human. I've worked as a research technician, laboratory manager with expanded responsibilities like biological and chemical safety officer, and as an operational excellence consultant in a *Fast Company* Top 5 "most innovative" company, alongside U.S. Top 10 and Global Top 20 biopharma companies—long enough to know that operational dysfunction isn't always loud. It doesn't wave its arms or send out press releases. It creeps in slowly, showing up as missed deadlines, vague responsibilities, or reporting requirements that nobody truly understands.

The thing is, most people see the dysfunction, but everyone ignores it. Academic research was a little different. Different in the sense that you were the writer of your own journey. You had research goals supported by the PI and kept a heads-down focus on what you needed to accomplish for your qualifying exam and PhD candidacy.

But the industry roles are full of handoffs from one group to another—a machine generating data and content while exchanging hands across the aisles and top down through the organization. Not always successfully, I might add. Communication is another area that becomes a challenge as organizations change through events like reorgs, mergers, and staff reductions.

As a former athlete and coach, I believe in the essence of teamwork. It's a lot harder to play the game when you don't know the people on your team. The better we know our teammates, the more informed we are on their expertise, roles, and capabilities. It requires an intentional effort to understand the network that is the organization—it doesn't just happen because we report to work. We have to lead with curiosity. These relationships also provide opportunities to grow. You are essentially developing a network of knowledge bases from the experts you have surrounded yourself with.

In the same vein, I noticed how inefficient things were. Not everyone played well with others. Conflict showed up in different places, sometimes in public, other times through relationships that kept you in the loop. You can learn a lot about how a place runs when there's conflict.

Aside from communication hurdles contributing to the conflict, there were patterns that would emerge. Thinking back, my first-year MBA course in organizational behavior (OB) primed me to see beyond the top layer. In many cases, conflict was less about the people involved and more about a broken process. Simply put, there was no communication on expectations, or how to do critical pieces of the workflow. Perhaps it was the scientist in me, looking for a protocol for how I am expected to run critical workflows. But workflow wasn't the only place where communication was lacking. As you'll see in this book, I've seen the same challenges pop up throughout this industry.

INTRODUCTION

THERE IS NO way to pinpoint the moment of realization that perhaps there was more to building a great biopharma company than any one method can provide. However, there are moments over the course of my experiences that showed me glimpses of how things are connected, glimpses of principles and management styles that worked, and others that didn't. One thing became clear: We don't always know what to call something, especially when it transcends traditional naming or workplace architecture.

There are a million and one ways to run a business. A million more to run one in biopharma—an industry that extends from medical device companies, pharmaceuticals, and biotechnology, through the contract research organizations (CROs) and other service providers that support the industry. When you consider the exits (licensing, mergers, acquisitions, outright selling) even more strategies come to mind. In an industry baked in research, strategy, intelligence, and unique and specific skillsets, we also find ourselves in an industry riddled with inefficiencies. An industry where the pace of science and technology outpaces that of a given workforce. The solution doesn't lie in robotics or artificial intelligence. The solution lies in the collective understanding of the organization, its people, its resources, the corporate initiatives, the future of the organization, and the management and social culture at the organization.

Bridging those gaps requires a different line of questioning than "what can make my organization efficient?" Or "how can we address our operational risk?" And sometimes the line of questioning is less professional, such as, "If this machine stops working are we screwed?" It requires a level of empathy, creativity, curiosity, and conviction to develop the right solution for the organization. And the same can be said for smaller teams or functions that act more independently and are responsible for their set of resources, training, onboarding, and project management.

This is where the Biopharma Nexus Model comes in.[1] My compilation of theories and consolidated principles focus on the key major responsibilities for developing connections in complex industries. Those connections grant you visibility into data and support for the development of insights that previously were left as unanswered questions. I developed this model to structure and visualize my understanding of, and approach for solving, major complex challenges, and addressing the operational risks that I have experienced in this complex industry.

Have you ever asked that "next-level question" during meetings with colleagues? Not the surface-level question on a status

1 The Biopharma Nexus Model is a map for structuring and developing key organization functions to expose operational risks and enable continuous insights throughout the development lifecycle.

or specific outcome, but one that digs into the strategy behind a decision. "Do we know where our resources are being drained and why?" "Is there going to be regular training after we start up this new system we're adopting?" If you have ever asked "the next question" be it at the organizational level, project level, or function level, and the response is "we don't know" or "not sure," then you are likely underleveraging whatever data or resources you have at your disposal to answer the question. In a battle of pace, science and technology will always outpace the development of our workforce. It is our responsibility to bridge that gap and eliminate any operational risk from the company. That link is what this meta framework is about.

This book explores this meta framework through the lens of biopharma, my direct experience. The successes over the course of my career have been attributed to tools, techniques, and mindsets that transcend specific industries. The stories you will find in this book are mostly from the biopharma industry—science, research, asset development, manufacturing, the works. The principles of the Biopharma Nexus Model pave a future for any complex industry that combines people, culture, resources, and strategic planning on a timeline that eventually leads into regulated spaces. This model is intended to become a tool for thought leadership in any organization or team.

The ongoing successes described in this book cannot be downplayed, as they extend beyond any return on investment (ROI) metric or balance sheet line item. This book considers the culture and mindset required at all levels to develop the well-oiled operations we all hope to walk into from day one on the job.

HOW TO APPROACH THIS BOOK

This book was not written to be read once and placed on a shelf. It's designed to live alongside your work—messy, fast-moving, and filled with nuance. Whether you're a leader in biopharma operations, a program manager trying to make sense of strategic disconnects, or a curious team member seeking clarity in a complex environment, *Predictably Broken* is your practical field guide.

Before diving in, pause and reflect on your current organizational landscape. What's making you uncomfortable? What's not quite broken, but close? Think about those near misses that don't get recorded but keep happening. Write them down. This book won't hand you a checklist to "fix" them, but it *will* give you new language, structures, and insights to help you examine what's underneath the surface.

I suggest reading through the book once to get familiar with the five pillars of the Biopharma Nexus framework. Let the concepts sit with you. Then return to specific chapters when you're facing challenges in those areas, whether it's misaligned governance, unclear decision-making processes, or siloed technology rollouts. You'll likely find something you missed the first time or a particular element that resonates differently as your context shifts.

This isn't a linear manual. It's a reflection tool—a place to return to when your team needs to slow down and ask, "Are we solving the right problem?" It's structured around real-world complexity—where project management philosophies like Agile might not cleanly apply, and where your ability to lead through uncertainty matters more than your job title.

Throughout this book, you'll find case studies woven into each chapter—some brief, others more detailed—that bring the Biopharma Nexus Model to life. These stories are drawn from real organizations—anonymized where necessary—and illustrate the operational patterns, pitfalls, and breakthroughs described in the text. They're not just illustrative—they're instructive. Whether the example comes from biopharma, academia, or adjacent complex industries, each case study is selected to show how core concepts play out in practice. Our goal is to ground theory in reality, helping you see the connection between strategic frameworks and day-to-day execution, and empowering you to adapt these lessons within your own context.

I wrote this book with real people and imperfect systems in mind. Expect some wit, honesty, and the occasional parenting analogy to help clarify high-stakes organizational dynamics. The stories and insights aren't just academic—they come from years of lived experience, mistakes, and hands-on experimentation across biopharma, research, and consulting.

This book is also designed to be shared. You may find yourself flagging sections for your team, offering a chapter to a colleague, or using it to spark a roundtable conversation at your next strategy offsite. Leaders can use it to frame challenges and re-engage teams. Consultants can use it to deepen their diagnostic thinking. Teams can use it to build a shared language around operational excellence and risk exposure.

Finally, you'll notice this book doesn't prescribe a single formula. That's intentional. It's not about perfection. It's about enabling thoughtful, strategic, and human-centered decision-making at every level of your organization. Because in biopharma—and any complex business—you're either trying to win or trying not to lose. This book helps you do both, with more clarity and less chaos.

To protect the confidentiality of the individuals and organizations involved, we have chosen to anonymize the names of all case study companies featured in this book. While the lessons and insights are drawn from real-world experiences, anonymization allows us to focus on the core challenges, decisions, and outcomes without compromising privacy or proprietary information. In some cases, details have been slightly modified to further ensure anonymity while preserving the integrity of the lessons shared.

WHY BIOPHARMA

People sometimes ask me: "Why biopharma? Couldn't this apply anywhere?" Sure, parts of it could. But biopharma has unique pressures. The regulatory environment is intense. Timelines are long and uncertain. The sheer nature of human biology, for example, can be relatively unpredictable. The high operational risk of running a capital- and resource-intensive business funded by preliminary data (relatively speaking) and a hypothesis that will evolve over the 10-year development lifecycle, is riddled with unchartered risk. And when you are eight years in, can your new discovery enable you to scale in manufacturing to reach the target patients? Teams are deeply specialized and often siloed. And yet the stakes couldn't be higher—people's health, safety, and lives depend on what we do.

There's also a strange paradox at play: the more technical the organization, the more human the breakdowns. Communication gaps, misaligned incentives, unclear ownership—these are the problems I see over and over again, most notably through handoffs, human or system level. The Biopharma Nexus Model doesn't promise to fix everything. But it does give us a shared language and structure to begin that work—together.

THE WEDGE

One of the metaphors that's stuck with me through all of this is the wedge. When I first started cementing the idea to move into consulting, I called my company Wedge Consulting Group—not because I thought of a pie chart, but because a wedge is one of six simple machines. By definition, they are simple mechanisms that can multiply force. You may recognize the other simple machines defined during the Renaissance: the lever, wheel and axle, pulley, inclined plane, and the screw, which also multiply force. The wedge, initially chosen for its ability to lift (operational excellence) and separate (process-improvement initiatives) into actionable change that sticks, rather than trying to boil the ocean. I believed that the path to better risk-resilient tools was to implement simple practices that can maximize impact. A wedge creates space. It's small, but powerful. And that's what wedges do in practice.

That's how I think of the Biopharma Nexus Model. It's not a 300-page operations manual. It's a simple set of guiding principles, applied jointly and consistently across critical functions—Research Operations, Portfolio Operations, Business Operations, and Governance—connected through a unified language. Each of those areas is a wedge—something we can examine on its own, with its own requirements, but can also be seen as part of a larger whole.

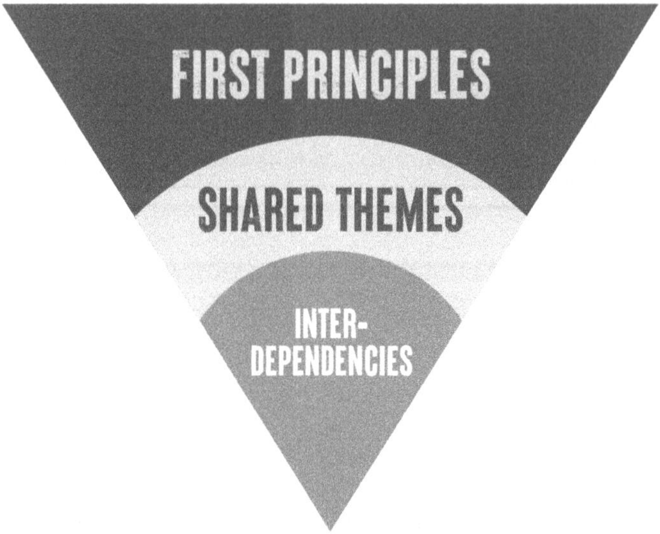

Each wedge has first principles. It shares themes and has interdependencies with other Nexus pillars. It's informed by real theory: lean, systems thinking, behavioral science, and capability maturity models. But it's grounded in real-world practice. That's the only way it works.

THE HUMAN ELEMENT

This book mentions and structures various frameworks and methodologies for identifying and mitigating operational risks. But don't mistake that structure for coldness. At the center of this model is people—your people. The ones trying to do their best work in systems that often make their work harder than it needs to be. Not because they want to, but because human nature is survival, even at work, and when decisions and responsibilities aren't clear and teams are left to their own devices to craft solutions, you will find yourself trekking through mud to make progress happen.

One of the core ideas in this book is reflection. It's not something we always make time for, but it's how experience becomes wisdom. During every engagement, I ask myself: What worked? What didn't? What sucked about this? What should we do more of next time? Where are the missed opportunities? Take the time to write something down. It doesn't have to be structured. It's free thinking on what transpired or didn't. Reflection is a space where many of us recognize its importance, but unfortunately, it doesn't ever seem to make the priority list over the tasks we have piling up. Reflection can show you the way to a better tomorrow.

The Biopharma Nexus Model is my answer to those questions. It's not perfect. It's still evolving. But it's real. And it works.

WHAT TO EXPECT IN THIS BOOK

In the chapters ahead, we'll explore each of the five pillars of the Biopharma Nexus Model in depth. We'll show you how dysfunction shows up in each area, what it looks like when it's working well, and how to start making meaningful change. Along the way, you'll hear stories from real biopharma companies—what they struggled with, how they tackled it, and what they learned in the process.

This isn't a prescriptive "playbook." It's a guide to thinking differently about how your organization operates, so that you can build one that doesn't just survive complexity, but actually thrives in it.

When reading, you will find references to theories and frameworks that have been utilized for decades, sometimes hundreds of years in some respect. We point out frameworks like Lean Six Sigma, an anchoring point for our journey through operations, driving a perspective of removing waste and delivering consistency as a means to approach operational excellence. We introduce systems theory that is a major contributor to how we understand our teams and organizations. All work is connected to other activities and support functions to deliver on company expectations.

The theories might also teach you something, and pause you to reflect, like the capability maturity model that describes company process maturity through phases of (software) development, over time. They depend on the capabilities of the organization and what has been developed internally to manage operations. On the low end of maturity you may find disjointed paperwork and activities, while on the high end you may find a fully loaded organization utilizing technology and upskilling to maintain themselves as a leader in their industry.

By no means is it an exhaustive list of everything that has ever influenced the Biopharma Nexus Model. Many frameworks may focus on problem-solving methods, or a stepwise approach to developing a strategy. The Biopharma Nexus is a map that brings together key aspects of these theories and frameworks, and redefines them in the context of biopharma and other complex industries.

WHOM THIS BOOK IS FOR

This book is written for senior leaders in the biopharma industry—particularly those navigating the operational complexity of growing companies. Whether you're a COO, functional head, or executive sponsor of cross-functional initiatives, you'll recognize the tension between scientific innovation and business execution. This book provides a clear roadmap for leaders who are tired of operational silos, unclear project ownership, and data chaos. It's designed for people who understand that operational excellence isn't just about improving systems—it's about building the connective tissue that helps teams work smarter, faster, and with greater strategic clarity.

It also speaks to rising stars within biopharma organizations—project managers, business operations leads, and cross-functional team members—who are hungry for frameworks that help them drive real change. These readers may not hold the top title yet, but they're deeply embedded in the execution layer and often see first-hand where things fall apart. For them, this book offers language, tools, and mental models to influence up and across the organization. It validates their experience, while offering them practical guidance to step into leadership with confidence and clarity.

Whether you are early in your career, managing a small team, or responsible for the operations in a 1,000+ employee company, there is something here for each of you. As my career advanced, and trust among colleagues grew, so did my exposure to, as well as my recognition and eventual understanding of, what separates "good" from "great!"

This book has three distinct audiences, and all of them will benefit from the theories and case studies explained throughout.

This book is for early career workers, which includes entry level roles where a majority of the work is foundational. These roles are for people new to the industry, whether they are new to the workforce or have transitioned between industries. In biopharma they could be analysts, assistants, representatives, and technicians—to name a few. My hope is that this book will reinvigorate your thirst for knowledge, and will prompt you to ask questions and not be silent in the face of internal chaos.

Open your mind to understanding the world around you. Develop your mindset to look beyond the task in front of you and ask yourself, "where does my work fit into the grand plan?" Show curiosity to everyone, not just your peers. Explore opportunities for side-quests to understand better how others execute their work at your organization.[2] I hope you feel empowered to come up with novel ideas in how you work and organize, and that you continue to iterate and refine, to support your work and that of your peers in the quest to support the organization's goals.

This book is for the middle manager. Becoming a middle manager is a challenging transition for some. Where your work used to be that of an individual contributor, you are now positioned to take the strategy (sometimes unclear) and develop actions for your team. I hope this book reframes your mindset and positions you to elevate the conversations you have with senior

---

2 Side-quests are tasks or initiatives that exist outside of your day-to-day work. They are usually introduced by leadership or someone with higher authority.

leadership, bringing the conversations into a strategic lens, while understanding the downstream impacts of isolated strategies.

The middle manager must begin developing a mindset that connects the broader strategic intent to the minutiae of activities scheduled over the course of the next project. In a challenging position, many will take the wishes of leadership and turn them into actionable moves. Rarely do we remove tasks and responsibilities from our plates, instead working for months on side-quests, brought on by unpredictable factors that drive us further away from executing the organization's priorities. After reading this book, I hope you feel empowered to speak up, and to own the challenges of the role and view it as an opportunity to become a conduit to shrinking the gap that becomes operational risk, and to feel empowered to speak the truth to power and to move mountains in a short time.

This book is also for the executive. My hope is that this book brings the perspective of an entrepreneurial mindset. A mindset baked in growth and not fixed positioning. A common theme when industry growth occurs, leaders from large, established corporations are often brought in to lead a new and emerging organization into their future. To the leaders, "innovation" cannot stay at the level of a chosen research domain—it must also include the internal team and resources.

If you have never built an organization from scratch, take this book and allow it to open the aperture of your perspective in how to grow a company together, systemically. Recognize that a culture of innovation and excellence cannot happen without the support of leadership as a true need. While innovation and excellence may seem to be "nice to have," operational exposure is not. This book will attempt to connect multiple stories across various functions and groups by similar themes in their challenges and how the solutions were designed. To the seasoned executive, this book will become a tool and a reminder of the role of people, process, technology, mindset, conviction, and curiosity in cultivating excellence.

WHY A NEXUS

Over time, I started to see a pattern. It wasn't just that companies were struggling with execution—they were struggling with alignment. The left hand didn't know what the right hand was doing. Legal was off in one corner, Finance in another, R&D somewhere else entirely. Then for leadership visibility, your entire team is required to piece together a presentation. The bigger the organization, the worse the fragmentation.

To support my own development and understanding, I started mapping what I saw. At first, it was practical: Who's responsible for what? What tools are they using? Where are the decisions being made—or not made? Those maps only created more questions. During that time, my interest in the business of biopharma grew, as my coursework became less about the tangible needs and more about the strategies, framework, and mindset needed to drive a successful business as a leader. Transitioning outside the laboratory transformed my work from a doer to a thinker. Building a company takes both. Over time, the maps I built became more conceptual. My work side-quests expanded my abilities as a doer and in testing the strategy I had learned during my MBA coursework.

I started learning about systems theory, Lean, Six Sigma, and organizational behavior. I was intentional in learning about different forms of project management. I was open to friends, family, and colleagues in the work I was involved with. This openness also delivered criticism and cynicism. It was as if a broken system was expected. Everyone had something to say, and no one did anything about it. Could this really be "industry work?" Put your head down and work, even if it's ridiculous. Believe it or not, it is ingrained in the very fabric of how we function through the education system. It becomes a natural feeling not to question when a more senior person is speaking. But that just wasn't me.

Being outspoken in the workplace is one thing that can put you on the spot. You become visible and available. It can bring a lot of attention in your direction, not always the kind you were hoping for. But it always comes with learnings. One thing I learned during my MBA was that the foundations of business came long before the existence of biotech and pharmaceuticals. With a goal of developing the right asset to turn a profit, while developing a successful business for growth through those assets, operational fitness takes a back seat.

As my coursework was aligned to Strategy and Entrepreneurship, I continued to consume knowledge from people who have done it before. Hours upon hours of entrepreneur stories, strategy tactics and frameworks, physical copies and books on tape on leadership, conflict, and professional and personal growth. In this stream of development, I also recognized that established practices and frameworks existed all over.

I borrowed from the worlds of engineering, manufacturing, project management, and organizational psychology. One thing was clear: Nothing was a good fit for the biopharma space. There was no universal footprint for running a successful biopharma organization. There was a push for efficiency, but no one would fully articulate what that meant and how to achieve it. Problems would arise, and bandages were applied. Everyone in organizations and across companies had their own ways of doing things. This fragmentation and misalignment of systems, processes, and people drove siloed solutions to near-daily issues. I noticed that people often looked to fixes where errors had been identified rather than where errors manifested. Those early days also showed me the cynicism of teams for driving improvement solutions.

Maybe I was naive, or perhaps I hadn't suffered enough disappointment at the hands of corporate solutions that fizzle out or cause more issues altogether. Addressing the operational dysfunction in biopharma became an opportunity for me. I could see the connections within the organization—the who, the what, the when, the why—all in a single process map. Then I realized: The solution to excellence is there. Amid the theories and frameworks that have existed across multiple industries and initiatives, we needed a way to weave in the relevant parts of diagnosing, developing, and adopting a mindset, behaviors, and tactics into the complexity of biopharma operations.

That's what the Biopharma Nexus Model is.

It's not a one-size-fits-all system. Think of risk and opportunity as bedfellows. The way to achieve their mutual existence is to find each risk and seize the opportunity to improve, and to create a diagnostic, a conversation starter, and a roadmap for transformation. Recognize that biopharma companies are complex and adaptive systems—composed of people, processes, technologies, and values that constantly shift in response to internal and external pressures. All of those areas mean that our operational solutions can't be linear. They, and the approaches to successfully implement improvements, must be holistic, iterative, agile, and human-centered.

WHAT THIS BOOK WILL HELP YOU DO

This book will help you bring clarity and structure to the chaos that often defines biopharma operations. If you've ever sat in a meeting where no one could agree on a timeline, or you've watched projects stall because nobody could access the right data, this book will give you a framework to diagnose those problems and do something about them. You'll learn how to spot the friction points that slow progress—whether in research, portfolio strategy, business, governance, or data—and use practical tools to streamline communication, clarify ownership, and make better, faster decisions across functions.

It will also help you break down silos and build real cross-functional alignment. Too often, teams operate in parallel but disconnected tracks—science pulling in one direction, operations in another, and leadership asking for updates that don't reflect reality. This book gives you the language, mindset, and step-by-step approach to bring those groups into sync. Whether you're managing research timelines, scaling a portfolio, or trying to get vendors and finance to speak the same language, the Biopharma Nexus Model shows you how to bridge the gaps and create systems that actually support the work—not slow it down.

Most importantly, this book will help you lead change—regardless of your title. Whether you're just getting started in your career or you're leading a growing organization, you'll walk away with strategies to implement meaningful improvements without needing permission from the top. You'll learn how to shift from reactive problem solving to proactive system design. And as your company scales, you'll have a repeatable model to return to—one that grows with you. This isn't about perfection, or process for process's sake. It's about building organizations where people can thrive, science can flourish, and strategy turns into execution.

WHY WE NEED A NEW MODEL IN BIOPHARMA

Biopharma companies operate in one of the most innovative, fast-paced, and complex industries in the world. Yet, if you've ever sat inside a project meeting, tried to coordinate across departments, or onboarded a vendor, you know that the internal workings of these companies often feel like controlled chaos.

With millions of dollars on the line and life-changing treatments in development, many of the critical systems that support this work—project tracking, governance, cross-functional decision-making—are duct-taped together, inconsistent, or absent altogether.

That's where *Biopharma Nexus Model* comes in.

This model wasn't born out of theory alone. It emerged from the frontlines—inside the research labs, the clinical trial ops teams, the high-stakes budget meetings, the leadership boardrooms, and my very own entrepreneurship journey. Over more than a decade and a half of working inside academia, biopharma companies—from scrappy start-ups to growth-stage biotech firms to established therapeutic organizations—I saw the same structural issues arise again and again. People worked hard but couldn't see the impact of their effort. Teams operated in silos. Critical decisions were delayed or made based on incomplete data. And change—real, systemic change—felt out of reach. If change was attempted, it usually ended in a fizzle months later after a poorly executed initiative, driven from the top down.

So many biopharma companies are struggling to pinpoint the source of their problems. Individual teams and team members get frustrated by lack of progress or how much time they spend looking for things, but no one is coming in with an outside perspective to help prioritize these problems and create an action plan for turning them around. My hope is that this book will help you pause, perhaps change your perspective, and empower you to create a workplace that is enjoyable with a culture of being a better organization each and every day.

THE BIOPHARMA NEXUS MODEL

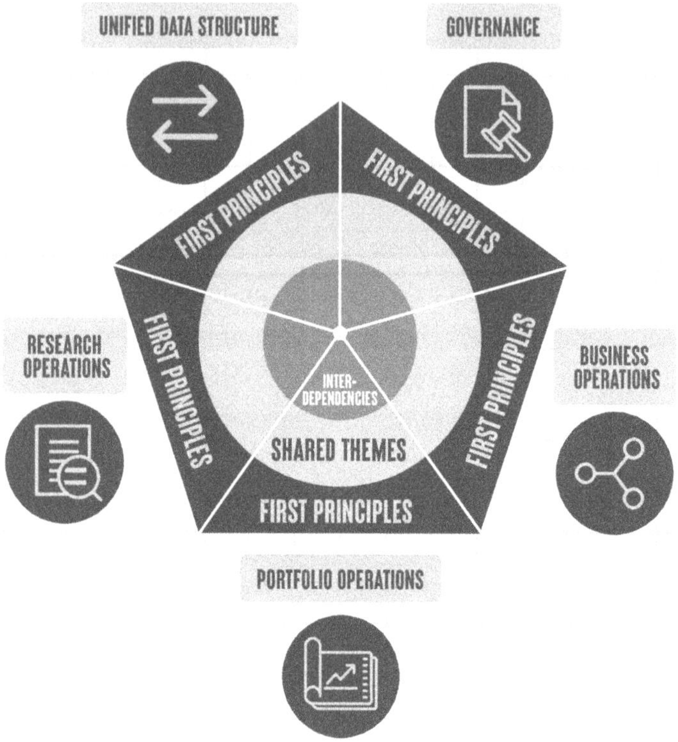

Let me take you through this model. At first glance, you'll notice that it is a pentagon representing the five pillars. Much of what this model proposes is a continuous feed of connectivity through these core pillars over the life of a successful organization. These pillars were the result of an evolution of thoughts about what was critical to limiting any operational risk exposure in the pursuit of excellence.

Recognizing that the structures of organizations can vary widely from how they are governed to the specific names of their functions and departments, this model represents the fundamental responsibilities in business that are the pillars of the Biopharma Nexus Model:

- Research Operations: How well are you developing your assets that will eventually provide revenue to the business? How do we protect that development from operational exposures like delays and resource consumption?
- Portfolio Operations: How well are you managing the progress of specific projects to advance your developing assets? Are you using the right resources on the right projects?
- Business Operations: How well are you managing your resources, people, technology, and funding?
- Governance: How will you organize? How will you make decisions? How will you empower your workforce?
- Unified Data Structure: What is your shared language?

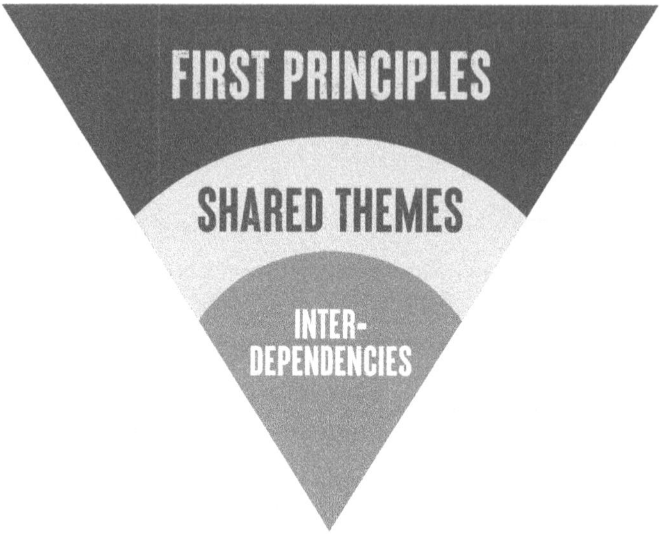

The model is divided into wedges that are subdivided into:

1. First Principles
2. Shared Themes
3. Interdependencies

First Principles of the Biopharma Nexus

The first principles of each wedge reflect the mindset to consider for each pillar. Each set of first principles directly addresses common challenges found within the pillar. The first principles may challenge a more conventional belief of that pillar, and that's okay. This model uses these first principles to anchor the perspective that explains why this model works. We will explore these principles further throughout the book.

Shared Themes

If the first principles are unique to the pillar, the shared themes are what bring them together. These are specific requirements at the organization level.

1. The pillars must own the development of their processes, and the integration, training, and socialization of the technology used within that pillar to the people across the organization.
2. The pillars must be aligned to the corporate objectives.
3. Corporate strategy is bridged through these pillars into action.
4. The pillars demand clarity of expectations from the organization.
5. Each pillar prioritizes continuous improvement and knowledge-sharing in the pursuit of eliminating risk and operational exposure that threaten the corporate objectives.

Interdependencies

Reflecting systems theory—which seeks to explain the interconnectedness of complex environments—the Biopharma Nexus views these pillars together, looking at the interactions and relationships between them, rather than developing and managing the pillars in isolation.[3] The activities and data that come from the interactions within each pillar can impact another, and therefore the model directly considers those relationships.

THE FIVE BIOPHARMA NEXUS PILLARS

Beginning with the Unified Data Structure (UDS), this pillar directly affects how data is labeled and flows across the organization.[4] It considers the different types of data that are characteristics of technical and non-technical roles. A UDS can connect the work being done to the project, task owners, resources utilized, even the flow of funding and expenses.

There are universal descriptors in many organizations. However, there are also ones unique to each organization, developed over time, that play a big role in the company culture and the language used internally to connect data across a complex system.

When data structure interdependencies are ignored, your ability for generating insights is diminished. Data that is disconnected from other Nexus pillars forces a translation in order to provide perspective and enable true data-driven decision-making. At the onset, it may seem obvious enough. However, when growth outpaces development, and new leaders and teams are empowered to decide how to execute, bringing everyone to the table to discuss a program can be an unwelcome reminder of just how segmented

---

3 Systems theory explains the interconnectedness of complex environments, focusing on the interactions and relationships of its elements.

4 Unified Data Structure (UDS) is the shared language and unified structure for all data points recorded at the organization that influence progress or insights. It is the strategic arrangement of data with consistent nomenclature across your organization.

the data is—especially when collating multiple functions into a cohesive story.

The ways in which a company makes decisions and how they organize themselves are known as governance. Governance is another pillar where the interdependencies may seem more obvious. In general, it is the responsibility of Governance to make decisions across the organization and cascade them to key stakeholders. Governance in the Biopharma Nexus Model focuses on how teams are organized, how decisions are made and communicated, and highlights their role in supporting the organization in achieving corporate goals—in this case, through an operational lens.

Collectively, all functions that support the work to develop a product or execute services are under the umbrella of Business Operations. Business Operations is the Nexus wedge with the widest responsibilities, with the target of supporting the organization's teams in their pursuit of executing corporate goals. The responsibilities and data acquired from this pillar directly affect the pace and capabilities of Portfolio Operations and Research Operations. It is where we bulk resource management, systems training requirements, legal and finance responsibilities that enable external resource support across the organization.

A successful company requires visibility into key activities that are driving its portfolio forward. The portfolio could consist of assets, products, experiments, projects, or clinical trials—to name a few. Portfolio Operations relies on transparent interdependencies across all Nexus pillars. This function is responsible for managing the planning and development of internal assets. Portfolio Operations in complex industries can also emulate a small business—managing teams and resources, budgets, and plans—in pursuit of executing specific and strategic goals. This Nexus wedge questions "are we doing the right projects?" And furthermore asks, "are we doing them in the best way?"

The testing of ideas and hypotheses are at the cornerstone of a complex industry. Data from these types of functions serves as a quantitative measure to successful development. In biopharma, Research Operations is at the forefront of generating data. It is imperative that the operations responsible for innovating and testing asset-development hypotheses have a clear path to their interdependencies across the other four pillars. As a resource-heavy wedge, it demands a close relationship to Business Operations. The scientific rigor to pursue development over many months and years requires an ease of translation of experimental results to broader insights that may impact all other pillars. It is a feedback loop that gathers its rhythm from successful execution and communication vertically and horizontally across the organization.

What can the Biopharma Nexus do for your organization, team, and own self? Transformation. This model intends to prompt awareness and reflection of your own career experiences and professional development. It moves us from a fixed to a growth mindset, shifting us into what's possible. It brings a systems approach, sharing not how we are different, but how we are connected, strengthening collaborations. It carves a path to real prioritization and away from fragmented information and gut feelings. It can act as a blueprint to a culture of accountability, transparency, and innovation through operations that are tailored to complex, risk-prone, innovation-driven organizations.

CHAPTER 1

CREATING THE BIOPHARMA NEXUS MODEL

AT THIS POINT, you might be asking, "Why do I go through the trouble?"

The answer has taken many forms over the years. At first, my effort was probably self-serving. Not living up to my own career expectations early on, I wanted to find a way to make a splash in my career. The autonomy of science work made me feel like I was in charge of my destiny. I wanted to make it easier to reach that end in my work. So, I took on "extra work" to design my day-to-day labors with as little friction as possible. I found that reducing friction required synchronicity. What I didn't expect was the blast radius of those improvements and changes by sharing the things I was working on with colleagues in the breakrooms over lunch. People became curious. Conversations continued, and showed me that when you get one or two people involved, their awareness slowly grows and branches to others.

In the end, improvements help all. What gifts to give others. Alignment—everyone actually knows what everyone is doing.

Pace—you gain momentum from having less friction. Impacts—to culture and to ways the teams remain connected and collaborative. All of those outcomes were possible because we chose to improve. The effect isn't just a moment in time. Like building any business or team, or improving your own work, it's a journey that demands a solid engine under the hood.

What makes the model that I created different? Its foundations are most certainly crowd-sourced. Some models and theories were derived from lived experiences. I may not have had a name for others until a few years ago. When I finally found my career path, the curiosity grew and was followed by understanding and time to reflect. My model—the Biopharma Nexus—is designed explicitly for the cross-functional messiness within complex industries. It recognizes the polarization of scientific freedom and operational control, integrating operations like legal and finance as major contributors.

Each pillar begins with first principles' questioning, a way of diagnosing internally rather than an off-the-shelf solution. This practice lends to the flexibility of the model, as opposed to a more prescriptive method. The model appeals to anyone, regardless of their background in operations. You can understand the model in a single visual and can go deeper to explore the layers.

Several models focus on the diagnosis or how to execute, such as PDCA (Plan, Do, Check, Act),[5] and even Lean[6] and Six

5 PDCA is a four-step process for carrying out improvement projects.

6 Lean is a systematic approach to eliminating seven forms of waste: Transportation, Inventory, Motion, Waiting, Over-Production, Over-Processing, and Defects. Originated from the Toyota Production System (Japan) in the 1930s.

Sigma[7] on their own. The Biopharma Nexus Model combines the right diagnostic lens with high-value tangibles and intangibles that are broken or misaligned. It takes you through the journey of awareness, alignment of people, processes, and systems. It recognizes that change is guaranteed, so adaptability is paramount.

The Biopharma Nexus Model came from my own direct experiences at the lab bench, in program management, and through my journey as an entrepreneur and life-long learner. I often heard that "[insert project management methodology] doesn't work in biopharma." Another criticism was that the methodologies and models available were very function-focused, thus siloing improvements. I have seen situations where siloing change only further fortifies a wall between teams. To bridge those issues, the Biopharma Nexus Model encourages a focus on high-value interdependencies, not just internal breakdowns.

Let me tell you what I experienced.

As my career has progressed, I held this internal feeling that the work I was doing couldn't be more obvious, bordering on the absurd. I was fixing issues that, in my opinion, should not have reached such a level of dysfunction. After all, my work was directly involved in unifying multimillion-dollar projects. I came into the industry assuming that everyone had their "*–ish*" together, to borrow a reference from a friend and one who is a leadership-conflict coach and is well respected. I had a touch of naivete. I quickly found out the *–ish* in my chosen career wasn't always together.

7 Six Sigma is a process improvement methodology developed in the 1980s by Motorola that focuses on eliminating defects and variability from production systems.

The interactions that I became a part of opened my eyes to the challenges faced by organizations that, simply put, no one was positioned to identify and resolve. In some cases, issues I pointed out went unnoticed. A number of experiences contributed to the challenges:

1. Employees were not empowered to tackle fixes or changes that spanned the organization cross-functionally.
2. Employees felt too busy with their day-to-day role to deal with fixing issues.
3. A general lack of recognition existed regarding the overall toll of poor process or alignment in an organization.
4. "Not my role" was a common statement from employees who were direct stakeholders in the workflow.
5. Communication barriers were present that prevented beneficial outcomes—some the result of a strict hierarchical operations framework—resulting in a barrage of venting after a project meeting, rather than a candid discussion with all parties in the meeting.
6. Budgeting workflows that would take two months to develop, and another month to approve, were common.
7. Vendor onboarding practices that would take weeks to implement were a source of discontent.
8. Role expectations that were communicated through venting during other meetings, rather than connecting directly with the process owner, were not addressed.

I saw too much of the "staying in my lane" mentality. There was no empowerment for people to speak up. Any forward movement was driven by leadership. Frustration for bad processes was seen as a failure of the process owners, when in reality they may have been doing just what they were instructed to do. All in all, people didn't communicate. They put their heads down, focused only on what was in front of them, and ignored the friction.

In these moments, I found myself not as a process owner, but as a bystander, asking myself, "if it's so bad, why doesn't anyone do anything about it?"

Well, let's digest the answer for a moment. We would need to accurately identify where the issue is, bring along primary stakeholders, develop and pilot solutions, launch the change, and maintain the change through training and other adoption efforts. So, perhaps those requirements are the reason why issues go largely unaddressed until they cause a huge ripple. Each challenge contributes to the feeling that everything is on fire, always. While you're putting out one, there's a small "garbage fire" that's lurking in the office.

So, who can do something about it?

You. As a leader, middle manager, or even someone who is early in their career, you can create meaningful change in an organization.

This book is full of my learnings over the years. It brings tested theories from multiple industries and initiatives, focuses on the human-centered aspect of what makes organizations flow, and considers the short- and long-term organizational strategy that becomes a North Star, guiding the planning, execution, and stakeholder radius.

For those who are early in their careers, this framework is much less about your role or title at the organization. As you navigate through this book, look at the examples. Ask how poor processes affect your own work, the team, and the project. Learn from the theory to develop a growth versus fixed mindset. Learn how to develop expert questioning skills to really drive to the crux of an issue. Develop a sense of awareness of successful frameworks across industries. Let this book guide you to an understanding of efficiency that drives value—not just to yourself, but to others around you as well. Become a mini entrepreneur and develop enough of a business mindset to understand what the organization cares about.

For those who are middle managers, you are in an interesting position to correct inefficiency and to advance the organization. Your spot in the company often stems from a high level of expertise and skill coupled with characteristics of a people manager. You have a budding strategic perspective. Middle managers have unique roles in that they absorb the strategic vision of company leadership and translate the objectives into action through their teams.

If that sounds like you, this book is also for you. My hope for middle managers is that you continue to grow. Growth from the theories and frameworks, recognition of all the cogs for a chance at successful operations, and empowerment to expand your relationships internally that will provide a continuing stream of expanded consciousness and knowledge to strategize and execute change. Pilot change within your team, and teach others of your learnings and successes. Show results across teams and departments, and create the FOMO for well-oiled operations. Empower your team to be involved in developing better systems and processes. This book will guide you in aligning with your leadership.

At the upper tiers, leaders should come in with a curious mindset. In many cases, leaders have excelled in their role through top positions with very focused work. This book will test you to expand your horizons. Successful change requires leadership support—more of support than enablement. Use the theory in this book that will provide foundations for the various stages of developing a Biopharma Nexus organization or team.

This book will point to proven strategies across industries that directly affect the people, processes, technology, culture, and mindset to successfully execute on improvement and risk-mitigation projects. It is the role of leadership to have clarity in their vision and to communicate that vision to the organization. My hope is that by reading this book, you, as a leader, reflect on the missed opportunities in your past and create a path to a better, more sustainable future.

THE PROBLEM: COMPLEXITY WITHOUT COHERENCE

Development of product in biopharma is inherently complex. At the highest level of product development, a business has to develop a concept, design it, build it, test it, verify it, and then make it accessible to the client/customer/patient. Each stage has its own relative timeline, budget, resources, and constraints.

How long will it take? How much will it cost? What do we have to do to make it happen? What are the rules we have to play by?

I think many would agree that the ability to answer those questions for a project can seem impossible. It's a typical "easier said than done" type of situation. But if you don't answer those questions, you're going to hit a wall and make some poor decisions.

Working in biopharma means juggling a strategy that is tied to your pace and cost to develop—especially if it is backed by venture capital or private equity. This makes sense. Why wouldn't a financer want to see their return earlier and on budget? You are betting on a 10-year cycle time and $2 billion investment to develop. A lot can happen in 10 years. A lot can happen over $2 billion, and not always the right things—a lot nonetheless.

Development stages can span a few months to a few years, working to refine your target product profile, iteratively developing the best product through hypothesis testing. All stages have their own processes, risks, scientific unknowns, skill or capability requirements, and resource needs.

If you want to move quickly, you can't develop every expertise in-house, so outsourcing becomes a major part of development. In most organizations, multiple projects are going on at the same time. Cross-functional teams, all with their own skill sets, capabilities, and work product, are employed. Keeping track of all those details amid the uniqueness of the output is more than a full-time job. Results, dates, tasks, owners, strategies, workplans, spending, and managing team dynamics can become challenging quickly.

Consider the volume of decisions that need to be made developing a drug product and the data to support those decisions.

Think of the coordination to start your first Phase III clinical trial with over 100 global sites and plans of enrolling 500 patients in a specific disease, therapeutic area, and patient population.

But complexity itself isn't the problem. It's the unmanaged complexity that creates risk.

In many biopharma companies, there's no single unified way to track projects and manage handoffs across functions. Cross-functional teams are composed of individuals from diverse backgrounds and expertise. They have their unique language to describe and capture their work. It's not unusual to see teams use different terms to describe the same initiative. Be aware that key data lives in disconnected systems, obscuring your ability to generate any kind of insight with confidence.

Governance frameworks are either bloated or nonexistent. How are you going to make decisions? What do you need to know to make those decisions? Everyone is rowing, but not always in the same direction—or worse, not even in the same boat.

The irony? Most of these problems aren't new. But solving them requires more than applying the latest framework like SCRUM, Lean, or Six Sigma in isolation. Although those tools do have a lot to offer—and I'll touch on various elements from them throughout the book—it's not enough to take one framework and lay it over the existing operations of a biopharma company. Those tools weren't designed specifically for the biopharma context, and when companies try to force-fit them, their effectiveness often falls short in execution or adoption.

SCRUM origins date back to a 1986 *Harvard Business Review* article, "The New New Product Development Game," by Hirotaka Takeuchi of Harvard Business School and Ikujiro Nonaka of Hitotsubashi University in Tokyo. It has since been adopted heavily by software developers as a framework to pass work flexibly back and forth among the teams to experiment quickly. These theories were further adopted and evolved into what is known today as SCRUM by Ken Schwaber and Jeff Sutherland, creators of *The SCRUM Guide*.[8]

Lean—more specifically, lean manufacturing—was an evolution of innovative thinkers. The notion of developing a production flow was initially put into full motion in 1913 by Henry Ford, who is now seen as the father of modern production lines. As the production line hit snags to introduce variety in automobile production, an opportunity struck the minds of innovative thinkers across the pond.[9]

In the 1930s Kiichiro Toyoda and Taiichi Ohno, along with their team, took the vision of Henry Ford and advanced their thinking to develop the Toyota Production System (TPS). The TPS advanced the thinking from individual machines and systems to focusing on the flow of any one product through the entire system, mastering quick set-up of machinery and building machines fit for volume.[10]

---

8 Hirotaka Takeuchi and Ikujiro Nonaka, "The New New Product Development Game," *Harvard Business Review*, January 1986, https://hbr.org/1986/01/the-new-new-product-development-game; Sohrab Salimi, "The Origins of Scrum," Agile Academy, accessed September 5, 2025, https://www.agile-academy.com/en/foundations/the-origins-of-scrum/.

9 "A Brief of History of Lean," Lean Enterprise Institute, accessed August 30, 2025, https://www.lean.org/explore-lean/a-brief-history-of-lean/.

10 "A Brief of History of Lean."

Lean continues to see many forms of innovation, originating from the thinking of Henry Ford, Kiichiro Toyoda, and Taiichi Ohno.

Six Sigma was first introduced by Bill Smith at Motorola in 1986, positioned to address variability in high-volume production. The principles of Six Sigma are Define, Measure, Analyze, Improve, Control (DMAIC), a five-step process to achieve less than 3.4 defects per one million opportunities. Those steps are the framework for developing sustainable improvements, while continuously iterating on those improvements.[11]

Lean and Six Sigma were ultimately brought together into one, as complements to one another. With Lean's core mission to remove waste (*muda*) and Six Sigma's objective to reduce variability, the business owner in me saw their combination as fundamental to growing a successful business.

At a high level, waste costs the company resources and can lower morale. There's nothing more demoralizing than work that goes nowhere. Resources that do not provide value for their assigned work diminish the potential somewhere else. Productivity fades.

Those challenges aren't just theoretical—they play out in the real, day-to-day work of teams across every stage of the product lifecycle. Whether on the manufacturing floor or in early-stage research, the effects of misaligned efforts and unpredictable outcomes are deeply felt. As organizations evolve and their strategic

11 "History of Six Sigma," Six Sigma Online, accessed August 30, 2025, https://www.sixsigmaonline.org/six-sigma-history/.

focus sharpens, the tension between innovation and efficiency becomes more pronounced.

Regardless of one's work on an assembly line or in research and development, variability in work produced can (1) make success more difficult to forecast and predict, (2) create a large gap to effective knowledge transfer, (3) produce unequal talent skill sets, (4) diminish leadership and partnership trust, and (5) misalign corporate expectations.

The focus of an organization tends to shift as it evolves from a portfolio of possible products giving you "shots on goal," to balancing the likelihood of success with the potential for high ROI early on. In other words, you pay up front to get things in motion, and as the organization matures, its priorities become focused, sending ripples through it.

Considering the intense resource consumption, shifting regulations, and new technologies that can support or threaten years of development, success comes to those who develop products within the constraints of the known universe and can manage their resources—time, money, people, technology, and its infrastructures. That truth cannot be understated.

I believe there is a map to accomplish such success. I sought and created a new approach that respects the scientific rigor, regulatory nuance, and human dynamics of the industry.

THE ORIGIN: FIELD-TESTED, NOT JUST THEORIZED

The Biopharma Nexus Model was born over the years, using my real-life friction in the industry and those of the professional relationships I have built among my peers. The waypoints of the model come from threads of friction identified across dozens of projects, functions, companies, and hundreds of stakeholders who supported the development of new solutions and perspectives. At times, my approach started with a simple question: "Why does this project keep getting delayed?" Other times, discovery began with a full-blown crisis, like unearthing 10,000 unread compliance emails, or realizing that no one in the company could produce an accurate timeline for a $200 million portfolio.

Over time, patterns emerged. And finally, so did a structure that brought it together: a set of pillars representing the foundation for this new way of thinking.

I. **Research Operations**
II. **Portfolio Operations**
III. **Business Operations**
IV. **Governance**
V. **Unified Data Structure**

The first three pillars reflect stages of my career in laboratory research, program management, and, more recently, entrepreneurship. My experiences in each gave me perspective on governance and connectedness. Each of those areas represents a critical "wedge" in the organizational system, one that either drives performance or creates friction, depending on how well it is understood, designed, and managed. Together, all the pillars form a unified framework for diagnosing problems, simplifying systems, and enabling sustainable operational excellence. The pillars make up the Biopharma Nexus Model and are your key to unlocking next-level growth, a better work culture, and maximum efficiency.

A NEW KIND OF FRAMEWORK: THE BIOPHARMA NEXUS MODEL

This book is not just a collection of best practices. It's a lens—a way of thinking about how biopharma companies operate and where they get stuck. The Biopharma Nexus Model is grounded in established theories like systems thinking, lean operations, behavioral science, and change management. But it also acknowledges their limitations when used or considered in isolation.

What sets this model apart is its integration. Each pillar is explored not only as a stand-alone operational function but also in terms of its interdependence with the others. Throughout the book, we will return to shared themes: (1) alignment between people, process, and technology, (2) clarity in roles and decision-making, (3) the importance of feedback loops, and (4) the need for a consistent, interpretable data foundation.

We'll also introduce you to a simple but powerful three-part process for transformation within any complex organization, such as biopharma—namely:

1. **Detect & Diagnose**—Uncover the biggest threats to your operations. Understand

what's happening, where the friction lies, and what's contributing to the breakdown. This requires identification of the right problem while avoiding any distractions due to its symptoms.

2. **Contain & Simplify**—Neutralize any cascading operational risk. Reduce complexity to what's essential. Clarify decision rights, streamline communication, and design for usability. Simplify the process for all stakeholders.
3. **Fortify & Adopt**—Build systems that are not only documented, but embedded into how people actually work—sustainably and repeatably, enabling resilient operations in times of volatility or scale. Fortify the findings and adopt the transformation through institutional knowledge.

It isn't a one-and-done approach. As companies grow, they face new problems. Have you ever heard the phrase "more money, more problems?" It accurately describes how you might face a landscape of new problems as the company becomes more successful and scales up the number of employees and open projects. The Biopharma Nexus Model gives you a framework and three-step process you can return to again and again as you face challenges.

THE RIGHT MINDSET FOR REAL CHANGE

If you're reading this book, chances are you already suspect there's a better way. You might wonder why the requirements of your work are slowing you down, are messy, and are unscripted. Maybe you're a team lead who can't get a straight answer on cross-functional timelines. Maybe you're in operations, drowning in tools that don't talk to each other. Maybe you're a senior leader trying to scale without imploding your team's capacity. Or maybe you're just tired of solving the same fires every quarter.

You're not alone.

The work we do to fix these systems isn't glamorous. It's not something that shows up on a company balance sheet. It is a living part of the team and requires agility to build operational resilience as the organization is growing, or surviving. It's often behind the scenes, slow-moving, and requires patience and planning. It demands a baseline of internal support. It means reflecting on what's not working, finding the biggest risks to your operations, resisting the urge to patch and move on, investing your time in building with others, and doing the harder thing—fixing the root cause.

But this work is also incredibly rewarding. It empowers the development of the workforce, consisting of teams whose operations are resilient in times of uncertainty. Conversations shift from providing updates to focusing on the real challenges. Stakeholder pools start to expand as interested parties find themselves curious to connect. Friction that once drove a wedge between data accessibility and actionable insights is now a figment of how things once were. When implementation is done well, teams stop spinning their wheels. Strategy becomes visible. Execution has rhythm. And the organization begins to move in the same direction—together.

As we turn from leadership foundations to the people executing the work, let's explore how team alignment and culture form the engine of strategic growth.

Chapter 1 Takeaways

- Leadership is a mindset, not a title.
- Leadership in biopharma must be intentional, not reactive.
- The leader's mindset determines how risks and opportunities are framed.
- Trust is the currency of influence in any change initiative.
- Courageous leadership embraces uncertainty without sacrificing accountability.
- Strategic clarity begins with self-awareness.
- Setting a vision aligned with purpose is more important than perfecting execution early.
- Leaders must constantly examine how their own actions shape team culture.
- Follow the five pillars shown on page 31 to bring foundational impact across the organization.

CHAPTER 2

RESEARCH OPERATIONS–THE SEEDLING OF INNOVATION

INTRODUCTION: CREATING THE RIGHT ENVIRONMENT FOR SCIENTIFIC SUCCESS

MOST BIOPHARMA COMPANIES suffer from the same core misbelief that science alone is enough to drive innovation. Innovation has become synonymous with new technologies, new treatments, and reaching new patient populations that have never had a viable treatment. The truth? Scientific breakthroughs are fragile and rarely happen by accident. Breakthroughs that turn into impactful outcomes demand the right environment and careful orchestration of:

- Strategy - Why are you doing this work? What do you want to develop? How will you do it?
- Resources (money, people, technology, time) - How much time do you have? Who

are the people who will carry out the mission? Support the mission? What tools and technology will you provide? How much will it all cost?

- Processes - What are the internal processes staff should align on? The critical ones.
- Information - How will you organize all of the data produced? What information is critical to enable data decision-making?

This is the role of Research Operations: to provide the structured ecosystem that allows scientific creativity to flourish without being derailed by operational complexity that often leads to chaos. This is a foundational wedge and the scientific engine.

My own journey into this world started through university lab coursework in the early to mid-2000s. It continued through academic lab roles with hands-on research, at the forefront of early research and discovery, long before the research gets picked up by pharma to develop the next innovative therapy. As someone new to the lab—especially someone who wanted to leave their prints on human biology—there was nothing more exciting to me than the aspect of discovery. Finding something that, to your knowledge, had never been uncovered, truly provides a feeling of contribution to humankind. It was a humble reminder of how far we have come and how little we know.

It was at the end of my Biology degree when biomedical engineering caught my attention, influenced by my physics professor, an engineer by trade. That moment elevated my thinking behind what careers were possible through life sciences. Perhaps it was inevitable—my father spent 40 years at NASA, eventually leading campaigns like the Launch Abort System for the ORION capsule in the mid-2010s. Engineering and systems thinking were in my blood. And working in a lab framed that thinking in a whole new way.

Early experiences in academic labs taught me the basics of peer-reviewed research, experimental planning, and hypothesis testing. Those are the core skills for many people drawn to work in this industry. There, the scientific method becomes more than something learned in school for your end-of-year project. It wasn't until years later, after I moved into operations roles, that I really saw how much great research depends not just on smart science, but also on how well you manage timelines, budgets, people, and resources—it's all about your ability to make things run smoothly. All those experiences stacked together showed me how all the puzzle pieces fit together and led to major transformations in the companies and the stakeholders I've worked with since.

ACADEMIA TO INDUSTRY RESEARCH TRANSITION

In many large biopharma companies, research operations are both invisible and critical at the same time. In smaller companies, this function is left to the scientists to figure out. Many are bred through academic research, as individual contributors, working toward goals for their own projects. This experience creates a narrow window to see into collaborative research.

Internal industry initiatives that require multiple stakeholders with diverse expertise and roles involve an adjustment that can take years. Academic projects take on the pace of science, whereas projects in the industry take on the pace of leadership or project expectations. Laboratory managers may be the mitigating solution for many. But for those who are new or inexperienced, this additional role can be a mountain to manage.

Research operations enable scientists to focus on science, shield them from unnecessary distractions, and strategically steer scientific work to align with goals. When operations falter, the cracks show—experiments are delayed, data is misplaced or mislabeled, strategy stalls, and brilliant ideas are lost in the noise of louder voices or prettier data. In so many labs, there's a sense that something is missing, but it's hard for individual team members or leads to actually recognize that the cracks are due to research operations issues.

Industry expectations can feel impossible. Planning experiments months out, considering corporate research goals, building budgets for experimental plans so far into the future that you might as well use a Magic 8 Ball on the plan to get there, all while driving results for the "now"—the work directly in front of you that requires your full attention.

It doesn't always have to be that way. Following the Biopharma Nexus Model's framework for research operations can be a game-changer. It can lead to repeatable, consistent processes that enable scientific breakthroughs.

Creating this environment of culture, action, and transparency isn't about adding bureaucracy. It's about designing systems that quietly support researchers, removing friction points before they can slow down momentum. It's the difference between a garden that grows wildly and chaotically versus one that, through careful tending, produces abundant, healthy plants.

Importantly, research operations must recognize that scientific teams are not just laboratories—they are micro-business units.

In lieu of a research operations lead, through title or responsibilities, scientists today are expected to manage vendors, strategies, budgets, timelines, and deliverables—often without the formal training to do so. Supporting this "micro-business" mindset is a critical operational priority.

COMMON OPERATIONAL CHALLENGES IN RESEARCH

Not convinced that your team and organization are facing operational issues? They can be difficult to identify, especially when multiple problems occur at the same time. They may not appear to have a root cause or someone to point the finger at—an unfortunate by-product of having no process at all.

Operating effectively within biopharma research is not easy. Scientists must be supported, but they must also have the curiosity to understand how operations impact their work. The shift is from an individual contributor to a team contributor. Everyone on the team must be rowing in the same direction. Multiple moving pieces and stakeholders performing their specialized tasks, and work management, with synchronicity and alignment to project and corporate goals.

Over my years working in labs directly and as a consultant, I've noticed common patterns. These issues can vary in terms of their severity, duration, and impact radius, but all of them are indications of biopharma operational challenges.

Common operational problems include:

- lack of operational training
- fragmented communication and siloed teams
- unclear prioritization and strategy
- unsynchronized data
- duplication of work
- inefficient use of resources
- no clear timeline of ownership
- governance gaps
- low ROI on R&D investment
- burnout and attrition
- vendor issues and delays

Symptoms that your organization may be suffering from these issues include: (1) scientists struggling with project and vendor management, (2) leadership feeling disconnected from research timelines, (3) teams struggling to develop R&D plans because "we just don't know" given the waterfall nature of many scientific strategies, (4) difficulty retrieving historical data, (5) poor documentation, (6) unmonitored lab budgets, and (7) experiments planned without clear checkpoints.

Many of these challenges don't come about because of one catastrophic issue or team member. Instead, they resemble death by a thousand cuts. The result? A collection of poor habits, misaligned incentives, inadequate training, and a culture that prioritizes scientific output while overlooking operational rigor.

Without deliberate focus, even well-meaning teams create systems where operations are "nobody's job and everybody's job" at the same time—a recipe for inefficiency. For example, consider a monthly effort to consolidate project budgets, a responsibility often put onto a project manager. However, the initiative is to be driven by the finance team. Other functions are also responsible for providing their updates, only no one was formally trained on how they are expected to physically manage their budgets, nor in how it's documented or maintained. There is a "budget process," but one that only dictates timing for the initial build. Do you get started on your own accord? Or is the process triggered by the process owner, finance? What if we're contacted late and don't have enough time to consolidate the financials? Rather than a collective effort to manage, teams may look to a single person with project management qualities. These issues are made worse by team changes, transitions, and grey areas of responsibility and ownership, which can be motivated by some of the problems we've highlighted above. High turnover among researchers and post-docs further erodes institutional knowledge. And leaders who treat operations as "nice to have" rather than essential to reducing risk, operational success, and efficiency, serve only to compound the problem.

DIAGNOSING AND TRANSFORMING RESEARCH OPERATIONS

Transformation truly begins with a shift in mindset, one person to lead it and others to participate. The right strategy and a well-delivered execution only work when the people on the other side are on board. And that outcome means shifting from a fixed to a growth mindset. From an individual contributor mindset to a part of a system, a living and breathing system. From a fixed mindset, where things just are the way they are, to a mindset of growth and continuous learning. A place where there is a future of possibilities.

This isn't your fifth-grade science project here. We're talking full-scale transformation potential. To lead successful transformation, having a systems mindset with considerations for stakeholders is key. To participate successfully, you have to embrace the feeling that change brings, widen your perspective, and transform to a growth mindset inviting that change.

Successful transformation follows a pattern I call "Nexus Transformation." This pattern originated from earlier work with my business partner, classmate, and long-time friend.

- **Detect & Diagnose:** Uncover your biggest operational risks. Understand where fragmentation exists—in data, processes, technologies, and cultures. What are the key features that directly impact the goals of the organization or team?
- **Contain & Simplify:** Neutralize any cascading operational risks. Streamline workflows, eliminate redundancies, and align systems. Remain focused on "why,"

enabling a closer view to simplification strategies that directly support the desired future state.

- **Fortify & Adopt:** Enable operational resilience through times of volatility and scaling by supporting teams through the change process with training, clear governance, and change management. Successful change is not forced. It is not performed behind a screen. It is the collective engagement and training of stakeholders who will become champions of change.

When organizations invest in this framework, the payoffs can be substantial: higher morale, leadership clarity, stronger skill sets, faster decision-making, and the ability to truly operate as a learning, adaptive organization. Executed correctly, teams gain a deeper understanding of the work they do and a wider perspective and vision on their contribution to the greater organization. Organizations will find better breakthroughs and happier team members who stay in place long-term.

HOW TO STRUCTURE RESEARCH OPERATIONS FOR INNOVATION IN BIOPHARMA

Research without structure risks becoming an academic exercise. Yet, structure without flexibility can strangle creativity and innovation. Academic research often aims to understand and explain the foundational truths of science that may have not been previously elucidated. It combines flexibility with curiosity to drive answering fundamental questions of how, for example, a disease infiltrates human cells. It is research that drives toward understanding, rather than a profile of a specific target product.

One of the most common barriers to enabling innovation through operations is the lack of a shared definition of what innovation should look like structurally, procedurally, or culturally. Many organizations aim to "foster innovation," yet they rarely articulate what that phrase means in operational terms. Without clear goals, frameworks, or behavioral expectations, it becomes nearly impossible for research operations professionals to build the infrastructure or processes that support innovative outcomes. This lack of definition leads to misalignment, siloed initiatives, and wasted resources—ultimately stalling the very innovation companies seek to accelerate.

Here's a specific example of it in action:

An overly structured research project, such as synthesizing a peptide product aimed at producing a blood brain penetrating therapeutic, may ignore the physical or mechanistic constraints of the therapeutic type. Peptides are large molecules composed of amino acids that can range 500-5,000 kDa,[12] which pose a number of challenges as a therapeutic. Although they offer a number of benefits—from lower costs compared with biologics, to lower immunogenicity (its ability to provoke an immune response)—peptide-based therapeutics can often lose their secondary and tertiary structures, creating instability, among other issues. The question that needs to be addressed is "what other resources are available

12 A.J. Pereira et al., "Peptide-Based Therapeutics: Challenges and Solutions," *Medicinal Chemistry Research* 33 (2024): 1275–80, https://doi.org/10.1007/s00044-024-03269-1.

that may have different characteristics, more fit to the goal for a blood-brain penetrating molecule?"

This divide can be bridged by leveraging the Biopharma Nexus Model, because the framework is both flexible enough to support new discoveries while also driving progress in a clear, meaningful way.

NOT EVERYONE IS BUILT TO MANAGE OPERATIONS

One mistake that organizations often make is assuming that scientists, by virtue of their experience, can also manage resources, vendors, timelines, and data integrity without dedicated operational support or guidance. But operational excellence is a discipline of its own, requiring specific tools, frameworks, mindset, and cultural buy-in.

In reality, many scientists struggle with managing project budgets, timelines, and vendors. Planning becomes a painful reminder of the uncertainties in R&D, especially when strategies are implemented in a waterfall approach, where any negative or failed experiment can derail progress or stop it altogether.

During early research conducted through Sigma Lab Consulting, we found that some academic investigators believed that training researchers to be fiscally responsible was not part of their remit. But if not the investigators training the next wave of industry scientists, then who? Without operational training, even talented scientists are left to navigate complex systems without a roadmap. The result? Many of the issues noted above—hindering progress and leading to internal team frustration.

Scientists already know the importance of innovation and discovery. But in order to achieve both, the right environment must be in place—one that recognizes accountability and responsibility.

Without operational infrastructure, even the best ideas can fail to materialize. How the data is layered, how the knowledge from your teams moves across groups within the company, and the tools and teams you use to support it, are all parts of the infrastructure.

Let's consider for a moment that every for-profit business either provides a service or a product.

McDonald's, Apple, Johnson & Johnson, all develop products for a customer base, their clients. Businesses like Amazon Web Services (AWS), FedEx, IBM, provide services to support the requirements or initiatives of other businesses or consumers. Many have long adopted a combination of products and services—from companies that help maintain your laboratory clients, to other services like environmental health and safety, genomic screening, R&D consulting, regulatory submission support, and outsourced manufacturing to name a few. Businesses provide something to a client or customer in return for money, a product, or a service.

When I was 18, I took a job as a pool manager for a public swimming pool in my hometown. They had a formal board and some staff, with the lifeguards being the largest team, who reported to me. Being the most senior full-time person, it was my responsibility to ensure the health and safety of the water, among other things. That task was a main checkpoint for the health inspector that would come, unannounced, to audit our pool. Even as a public pool, it had a regulatory body that enforced our baseline constraints for providing services. The same could be said for starting a consulting firm.

Each business has some regulatory body with a set of baseline requirements that it must meet to provide their service or product. These baselines, among other reasons, attempt to create a "level" playing ground for others in the same industry.

In this context, at any time, any business is typically looking to understand:

1. Are we doing the right things? Are we working on the right projects?
2. How much money are we spending on each project?
3. How much staff and resources do they take up?
4. Where do we outsource? What is that impact on the business?
5. What external circumstances could change our positioning or approach?
6. How can we do more?

They'll ask, "How much longer do we expect the project to continue, and are we adequately resourced to support that?" "Are we utilizing the right people, on the right projects and initiatives, and doing the right spending to achieve our operational goals?" The answers demand an infrastructure to view how time, money, headcount, and progress are connected within your team or organization.

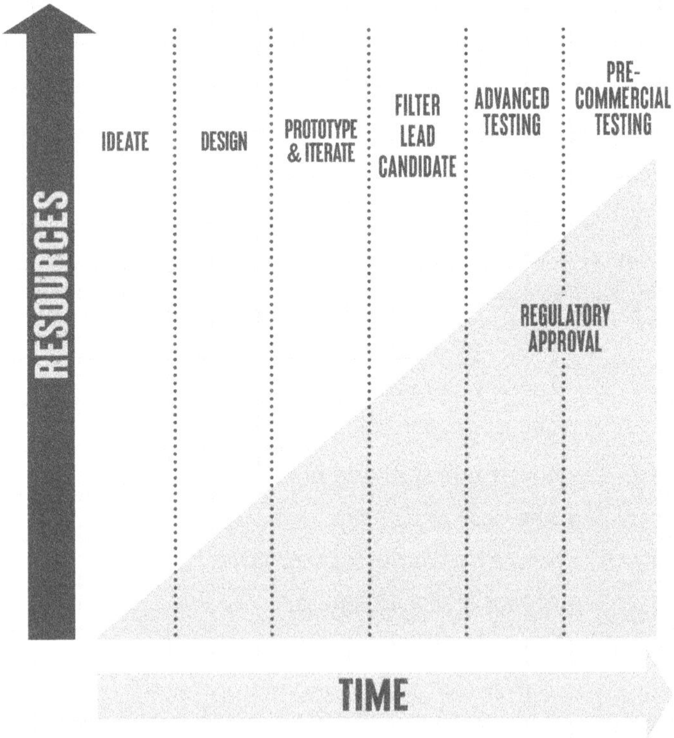

Typical progression from an idea to early human-testing data for a product. As time advances the resource needs increase, owing to the complex nature of product development.

Complex businesses demand well-designed operational infrastructures, from how you record your execution to how you manage a budget. It is widely known that more investment to cover research expenses is required as the projects move through major development phases.

Without the right infrastructure, experiments run over budget or behind schedule. Teams spend more time chasing down information than analyzing results. Talent is burned out by inefficiencies rather than inspired by progress. Projections and planning become high-risk activities, loaded with wishful thinking and linear strategies that do not fully encompass the risks in novel approaches.

In my 15 years working with multiple academic institutions and pioneering biopharma companies in various capacities, I've seen firsthand how quickly things can break down without operational support. What was once seen as a luxury for mature organizations has turned into a standard, such as integrating operations professionals earlier in the pipeline of development. Many examples come to mind, but my experience at Innovations Biotech further amplified the reality that the pace of portfolio development can quickly surpass that of operational systems to manage it.

When I think about structuring research operations for innovation in biopharma, one of the biggest gaps I see is how underdeveloped the operational side of R&D really is. In my experience, most scientists come into industry straight from academic environments where they've had total control over their projects—timelines, pacing, even budgets, in a very loose sense. There's no real emphasis on collaborative planning, no requirement to track budgets closely, and very little cross-functional coordination—a by-product of how early scientific expertise in the industry is measured and reported. That mindset doesn't transition well to industry.

In the corporate setting, your work is just one piece of a much larger purpose.

In academia, the primary goal of the research is typically scientific contributions and knowledge. A Principal Investigator, whose research is often funded by grants, with a portion going to the university, leads the laboratory's research direction. The published data, lending to the credibility of the research and its investigator, providing for future opportunities.

Industry research travels through a different lens. Early research ideas are vetted for purpose and market value. The goal is to develop a target product, that will serve a patient population—the customer. These businesses look to build sustainable portfolios that continue to provide a source of revenue. Research has very different purposes between academic and industry worlds.

In all areas of business, workers perform tasks to either execute corporate goals or support those who do, as seen in specialized functions, such as Marketing or Research compared to General Services & Administration (GS&A) corporate functions. Whether we are developing the next natural product or managing expenses, our work creates data points that enable insights into areas of operational exposure.

You're tasked to manage vendors, track timelines, plan for resourcing, and coordinate with other teams. But in most research settings, there's no formal work management structure to support operations. Scientists might have access to laboratory information management systems (LIMS) or electronic lab notebooks (ELNs), but those tools are for capturing data and registering samples, not for planning or tracking operational progress. Who contacts possible vendors to understand their lead time? Who verifies the budget for the new wave of external work? In what format and how is the data going to be integrated?

Lab managers often handle logistics—like ordering supplies, shipping biologics, or maintaining safety protocols—but no one is truly overseeing operational planning within the R&D function itself. That's a huge blind spot. We don't teach scientists how to manage projects, and yet we expect them to operate seamlessly within these complex environments. The results are disconnection, miscommunication, and a lot of inefficiency.

What I'm advocating for in this book is a shift. We need to redefine what it means to work in research operations. Scientists don't need to become project managers, but they do need to have a basic understanding of how their timelines, budgets, and resource decisions affect the bigger picture. They need to know how to plan—not just experiment by experiment, but with an awareness of cross-functional dependencies.

That kind of operational alignment doesn't exist naturally in most research organizations, but it's absolutely critical if we want to be innovative at scale. It's not enough to just generate great data. You also have to be able to move that data through a larger system, and that aspect requires thoughtful, structured operations within R&D itself. That's the shift I think we need to push for.

When I first arrived at Natural Medicines, for example, project documentation was scattered across inconsistent Word documents, filed haphazardly into folder structures that varied wildly depending on who created them. There was no centralized visibility into project timelines, no system for tracking actions or decisions, and minimal alignment between project milestones and broader portfolio goals. Upon arriving, I realized that I was their first ever project manager.

In so many of the teams, the pattern was clear: The scientists on the team had brilliant minds and great potential, but there was only so much they could achieve within a broken, incomplete, operational system. The data was there, but the conversations were muddied because we couldn't see where we were going.

In this case, it came down to choosing the right tool that could address gaps and scale with the organization, and then getting the team to weigh in. It's important to note that there is no one tool that works for every single company. The key thing to remember here is that choosing the right tool and getting it set up properly for the entire team is a game-changer.

Here, we used the base infrastructure of the company and built the management of it using an existing enterprise software system. This tool created the foundation for strong research operations and communication across teams, and it was a tool the team could grow with.

The work management tool helped R&D to link meeting details, team goals, research timelines, decision records, and action items in one place. It sounds almost too simple to be true, but so many biopharma companies are missing that connectedness. By implementing the solution gradually and strategically, we were able to shift the research programs from a fragmented approach to a connected, streamlined, and organized operation. Not only did project management become a whole lot easier, but the scientists on the team got their time back to focus on their research, knowing we had a place to bring together and understand the risks and progress.

Truthfully, though, the change fostered something even more important and far-reaching: a culture of ownership, transparency, and accountability. With more easily accessible and reliable information, teams are able to move faster, more intentionally, and to collaborate more effectively. Conversations began with views made by reports, focusing on the things that demanded attention—an advancement from "what's on the agenda today?"

One thing, however, can strengthen the extent to which the team buys in or feels the change. And that's ensuring that the operational changes are made considering how people work, while being mindful of corporate goals and their impact. Without it, change feels good, but that change could be going in the wrong direction. Without considering the people, your change becomes a nice exercise that fizzles out after three months—maybe sooner.

ALIGNING SCIENTIFIC WORK WITH CORPORATE GOALS

Scientific excellence is necessary in biopharma. It's at the core of everything we do. But it's not enough. For biopharma companies, strategic priorities must also align with operations. Without both aspects, even groundbreaking discoveries can flounder before they achieve their full potential with development or commercial release.

Research operations teams help bridge this gap by ensuring that decisions regarding experimental planning, risk assessments, and resource allocation are made with corporate objectives in mind. It's not just about "doing good science"—it's about doing the *right* science.

Alignment also means anticipating what will be needed downstream: regulatory documentation, reproducibility of results, and scalability of experimental systems. Operational teams ensure that researchers don't just focus on short-term experimental wins that look good in the moment, but that the work also contributes to the long-term strategic trajectory of the company. Nothing exists within a vacuum, and all the pieces must work together under the bigger umbrella of corporate goals.

Yet, too often, companies operate in reverse—asking for individual department goals before setting clear corporate goals, or asking for budgets before goals have been made clear. Such backward planning creates chaos downstream. The reality is that teams will generate proposal goals based on their understanding of what a project may deliver in the following 12 months, usually pointing to a milestone. This short-term projection creates a diluted view of the work of this critical function. In the end, teams wind up with misaligned projects, fragmented budgets, and disjointed decisions. What's the purpose of turning in goals directed toward checkboxes but not rooted in strategy? When illogical direction leads, teams also feel unappreciated since they too don't feel recognized for the hard work that they put into meeting those team goals, however misdirected it might be.

So, before you can even look at the team level, you need the right order of operations: corporate vision first, with programs, projects, and functional alignment to follow.

The financial investment is high. In 2024, Massachusetts saw nearly $8 billion in venture capital funding invested into early-stage companies, with a majority going into R&D. Over 56% occurred in pre-clinical companies. Even mature companies can see 10%–25% of their total revenue positioned for R&D.[13] The sheer scale of this investment highlights the real impact of getting research operations in order.

The reality is, in complex industries like biopharma, your work is part of something bigger. You're one piece in a highly complex process that involves multiple functions, stakeholders, and deliverables. And you're expected to plan for timelines, think about risk, and be responsive to corporate needs. It's not enough to say, "we'll see what the data tells us." That timeline doesn't work

13 "2024 Massachusetts Biopharma Funding and Pipeline Report" (MassBio, 2024), https://www.massbio.org/wp-content/uploads/2025/01/2024_BiopharmaFundingReport.pdf.

when other teams are trying to plan manufacturing, regulatory, or partnership activities.

My early work at Natural Medicines involved mapping existing workflows to understand bottlenecks and points of friction. I also needed something on which to base a timeline, since nothing existed. What I ended up with was a workflow from screening to validation, spanning roughly six months of time, across seven distinct research functions. All in all, the workflow had greater than 100 steps, checkpoints, and decisions. In many cases I heard, "I had no idea" from direct stakeholders of the workflow, speaking to the breadth and complexity of their operations.

So, I believe part of what we need to do is expand the culture of R&D work. Scientists should have some development measures for planning—not just the science, but the execution as well. That knowledge should include anticipating how long it will take to complete studies, understanding procurement and vendor timelines, and being able to communicate realistic projections. We can't hide behind the uncertainty of the science anymore as a reason for poor execution. We have to get better at strategic planning in support of corporate goals, even in the face of ambiguity.

At the same time, I think leadership needs to understand that R&D milestones can't always be treated like product delivery deadlines. A better approach is to build strategic alignment by defining the parameters of success. What does progress look like? What are the minimum requirements to move an asset forward, and where can we be flexible? That way, both corporate and research functions are working toward the same goal, even if the exact pathway shifts.

My goal here is to show that aligning corporate goals with research execution isn't about forcing predictability into science. It's about creating shared language, expectations, and systems so that everyone is rowing in the same direction, even when the waters get rough. That's operational excellence in R&D, and it's something we have to be intentional about building.

To illustrate this, let's look at the work I did in my time working with Oncology Therapeutics, a company with fewer than 500 employees, with clinical trials in a variety of oncology indications, and with a single asset. You can think of its core business product as another attempt to match the success of Keytruda by Merck.

When I first joined the team as a lab manager in the mid-2010s, I felt like my whole job search experience was a lie. I spent hours per day, every gap of time, applying to roles in an effort to make my leap from academia to industry. I was often met with rejections due to a lack of industry experience as the deciding factor to forego my employment. Ultimately, I arrived at an industry role that didn't seem so "challenging." It had, what I thought was, complete autonomy.

I was also quick to recognize that the person I was brought in to replace had "checked out."—in the same office as mine, spending most of the day laughing from reading online posts and feeds. One thing I truly did not expect was the casual nature, doing just enough to keep the wheels spinning. It was as if everyone did things the way they felt like doing them—a recipe for unrepeatable data, inventory and resourcing fumbles, and budget overages. In other words, operational chaos.

Recalling my first inventory request, it came from hastily scribbled sticky notes with no vendor information or quality specifications. It was as vague as asking your spouse to go to the store and "buy food."

Labs were cluttered with costly, incorrect supplies that couldn't be returned. There was no systematic process for inventory management or resource forecasting. The team had no idea what their resource consumption was. Orders were made in the moment, as needed, including costly reagents. The routine meant the work on a given experiment began when the reagents finally made it to the lab.

With a new process and updated data, we prioritized consumables for bulk ordering, saving $15,000 on bulk ordering a single, commonly used reagent. Scientists were inadvertently wasting time and budgets because they lacked operational support.

Once I got the lay of the land, I knew that we needed to start with a better foundation in operations. Operations had to be valued just as much as the scientific work being completed every day. How you work every day is just as important as what you are doing.

By implementing structured procurement forms and inventory-tracking tools, we brought order to the chaos. For the first time, we had operational data. And that operational stability, those guardrails and adoption, freed up scientists to focus more on the actual science, improving the quality and speed of research outcomes.

Having operational systems in place also helped identify critical bottlenecks early. For example, tracking usage patterns allowed us to forecast supply shortages weeks in advance, avoiding costly project delays and rush purchases. This level of proactive planning only happens when operational thinking is embedded into the research environment.

Soon after starting this new role, I was plucked by executive management and positioned into a program management role. The same operational principles I applied to the lab were scaled up to portfolio management, supporting the company's first successful Phase III trial, followed by integrating newly developed systems across all active clinical trials. Did I mention it was as a team of one, just myself? It can be done—if you want it badly enough and have the support to back you.

PREVIEW: THE IMPORTANCE OF A UNIFIED DATA STRUCTURE

If there is a single foundation upon which successful research operations rest, it is a UDS—a common language that unifies the work being done, the results, the people who execute them, the projects that are impacted, and the resources it consumes. Without it, everything—from project reporting to budget forecasting and resourcing—becomes exponentially harder. We'll touch on this pillar more deeply in Chapter 6, but here's a quick overview so you can see how it fits into research operations.

If there's one problem I consistently see across companies, it's not communicating in the same language. A research team may have a specific project related to the formulation of a new drug, yet the financial budget may list "scalability experiments." Without a common nomenclature or domain expertise, this small difference will generate friction when it comes to matching up budgets to expenses. It will cue emails back and forth to reconcile where money was spent, for what purpose, and whether it was budgeted. This gap is often seen when using technical jargon in discussing our work with non-technical support. Why would they know what you're talking about?

New domains of research continue to drive the limits of innovation and discovery. This factor translates into complex cross-functional programs that merge multiple layers of expertise under a given team. True, there are some universal terminologies, but the details of our work like to take the form recognized by our domain of expertise. Not to discredit the role our experiences have taken in how we discuss our specific work to team members. These themes push roadblocks and hurdles right into the path of data transformation. That's what we want to get right—the data to tell us about the work we are doing. But the importance of being on the same page cannot be overlooked.

It can show up in many different ways, but there are a few I see most frequently.

Companies often fail to standardize naming conventions, workflows, or data outputs across departments or functions. As a result, different parts of the business call similar processes by different names, store information in different formats, and break critical data linkages. This disparity can look like different names for projects between a technical team and GS&A functions. Or managing a large cross-functional clinical trial where the clinical operations, chemistry manufacturing and control (CMC), legal, and finance teams refer to participating hospitals and clinics by last name, contract entity (often different from the actual name of a hospital or clinic), or even an internal ID designated for that trial site. The impact of this fragmentation can be significant and a silent roadblock of efficiency.

Fragmented communication and lack of standardization erode the organization's ability to

- roll up project and portfolio data accurately to keep projects on track
- make real-time, data-driven decisions
- forecast operational needs and identify issues effectively
- maintain institutional knowledge during turnover
- manage employee resourcing across active and upcoming projects

Those problems can be compounded when the integration of a new system is attempted without cross-functional collaboration. This dilemma occurs most often during planned scaling, expansions, or mergers. If there are any cracks with disconnected technology, they'll get inflamed during a merger, acquisition, or key leadership turnover.

I once consulted with a merged biopharma company where one half of the company called projects "initiatives" while the other called them "programs." Initiatives had four layers to express the roll-up from a task to the portfolio; programs had three. Seems similar enough, right? Wrong. Even basic changes in language and structure can lead to fragmented operations. The fragmentation seen there made it near impossible to craft a portfolio view, among other issues.

In this case, their chosen systems of use were incompatible. Each created their own datasets, using different systems to collect and manage the data, forcing manual reconciliation for even basic portfolio views. They lacked standard keys that connect data across systems and programs. It was clear: Without unified language and data structures, the company would never achieve operational excellence. Its operations would continue to pose a risk, missing valuable insights as to the health and status of operations. And there would be a gap that creates uncertainty as "progress" is made. The potential for driving real-time decision-making became a gargantuan effort and a pipe dream.

Investing early in common terminology and frameworks—for example, defining what is a "project," "program," or "initiative,"—and standardizing how those terms are tracked and labeled is critical. Every decision made about technology systems, operational processes, and governance models should reinforce this foundation and seek connectedness.

BRIDGING RESEARCH AND PORTFOLIO MANAGEMENT

Scientific projects do not exist only as a project or program in an individual department. Each experiment, each program, contributes to the broader organizational portfolio. Ensuring that research outputs effectively feed into portfolio decision-making requires intentional operational design.

Research operations play a critical role in that relationship. They connect the experimental work being done at the bench to the strategic decisions made at the boardroom table.

At one company I worked, they had "goals," but they were being developed in a less than effective manner during quarterly meetings. Ideas would cascade through the program teams and back up to program leadership. They would then connect input from partners and other stakeholders, while manually making presentation slide updates that eventually became the source of program goals, tucked away in some digital folder cloud space. Because quarterly meetings were seen as "update meetings," there was growing concern that introduction of new projects during scaling would suffer the fate of many programs—namely, "we just didn't have enough time for review."

One can imagine the cost and potential opportunities that are lost in having middle and senior leadership held in a meeting for multiple hours, hearing a majority of updates rather than utilizing the time with their leadership for critical discussions. One can imagine the opportunity cost of attending a meeting to discuss your progress, sitting for hours, only to finish the meeting without discussing the project, and with a request to provide a written update via email to leadership. Not a good use of time or energy. This is a practice that is the antithesis of operational excellence and a great example of introducing risk.

With Discovery Therapeutics in particular, we helped transform their quarterly goals review process from an exhausting three-hour in-person meeting into an efficient, largely virtual exercise. By coupling live project-level operational data, managed by the program managers, with centralized real-time dashboards, executives could access project status, risks, and milestones on demand. As a result, quarterly meetings shifted from being passive updates to active decision-making discussions, where leaders could focus on programs with critical risks and resource bottlenecks, while giving back time to those who were "operating as usual." Their system of use? One that already existed with active licenses yet underutilized.

The transformation, however focused, wasn't instantaneous. Initially, there was skepticism from primary stakeholders in transforming a process that was central to communications with leadership, and that everyone "knew how to do." But this initial revamp occurred over the course of weeks. It would involve review by program managers, various internal and external stakeholder meetings to align on the progress updates, connecting leadership to early views, adjusting presentations to leadership recommendations, reconnecting with stakeholders, and ultimately presenting their progress. Could this new process relieve the burden of the "dog and pony show?" The skepticism wasn't from only one group, but from all. Still, true transformation occurs before anything is built.

Transforming the mindset of teams from a fixed to a growth state will enable the acceptance of a better tomorrow, achieving the desired future state.

When we step out of our comfort zone of working through the madness and allow ourselves to grow intellectually and upskill at the same time, the path becomes clear. Leadership soon recognized the expertise of the group at a whole new level. Rather than jumping head-first, teams applied screenshots of automated reports, structured according to previous presentations so as to not shock the stakeholders or leadership. Meeting them where they were, was (and is) key to inviting leadership curiosity.

The system was not built as a replicate, but as an improvement on how information was collated, shared, and consumed. The automations and the resulting time saved, previously spent on multiple presentation versions, became icing on the cake.

Leaders recognized greater value in the ability to see real-time data, coupled with context, that eliminated the need to review programs that were operating "business as usual", and focusing on critical risks to programs. The new approach gained momentum with leadership, and more importantly with process owners and stakeholders.

So, what's the real impact of identifying these challenges and correcting them?

Identifying operational risk and striving for operational excellence at the portfolio level enables

- real-time status visibility across dozens of projects

- early identification of risk trends and resource conflicts
- faster pivots when strategic priorities change
- more efficient governance and decision-making processes
- teams to grow their strategic lens in relation to the work they produce

The net effect? Research teams can spend less time reporting and more time doing. Leadership can steer the organization more effectively through insights that were once available only after a month of manual exercises and email communications. And innovation can move forward at the pace the market demands.

FINAL THOUGHTS

Research operations are the silent engine behind biopharma innovation. They create the conditions for scientific creativity to thrive, align discovery work with corporate strategy, and bridge the gap between isolated experiments and meaningful portfolio impact.

If we want to nurture the seeds of innovation, we cannot focus solely on science. We must also cultivate the soil—the systems, processes, and practices—that allow those seeds to grow.

Organizations that identify and invest in research operations are the ones that will consistently translate good science into great medicines. They will be faster, more resilient, and better positioned to bring life-changing therapies to patients.

In the next chapter, we'll dive more deeply into how Business Operations can specifically support data-driven decision-making and experimental risk-management—two critical areas where many biopharma organizations still have room to grow. Business Operations build on the core research operations we've discussed here.

Building culture is essential, but it's only one part of the equation—let's now examine how we create clarity and momentum through well-oiled Portfolio Operations.

Chapter 2 Takeaways

- Team alignment requires more than structure. It demands shared purpose.
- Research requires thoughtful operations to enable flexibility.
- Empowered people make better decisions and take smarter risks.
- Teams look to leaders to carve the path to their goals, not the other way around.
- Culture is not what you say. It's what people experience every day.
- Emphasis on operations training can elevate technical roles.
- Leaders model the culture that they want to see.
- Be intentional in how you operate.

RESEARCH OPERATIONS

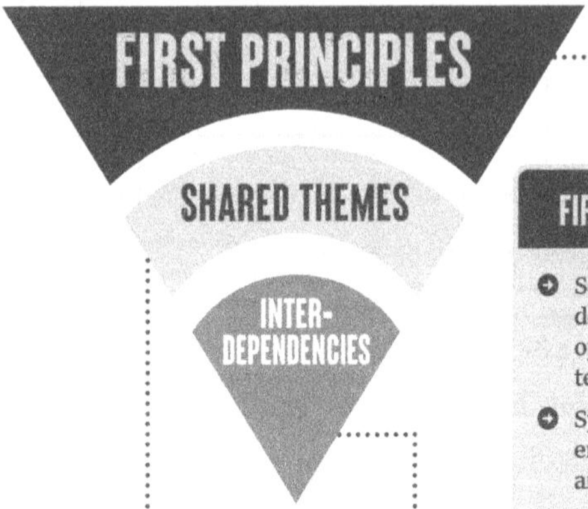

FIRST PRINCIPLES

- Scientific results depend on both operational rigor and technical skill.
- Systems—not memory—ensure data integrity and reproducibility.
- Funding should follow structured, prioritized workflows.
- Training and knowledge retention are as critical as design.

SHARED THEMES

- Own processes and tools through alignment and clarity.
- Connect operational discipline to corporate strategy.
- Maintain transparency, collaboration, and continuous learning.

INTER-DEPENDENCIES

- Informs Portfolio Ops on prioritization and research direction.
- Guides Business Ops on resource planning and investments.
- Grounds Governance decisions in real data.
- Provides technical language for UDS.

CHAPTER 3

PORTFOLIO OPERATIONS–BUILDING THE BACKBONE FOR BIOPHARMA EXECUTION

INTRODUCTION: LESSONS FROM THE BOAT

WHEN I REFLECTED on Portfolio Operations and my professional journey, there came the realization that my understanding didn't start in a boardroom. It began in a 40-foot crew shell on the James River. Rowing with the men's varsity team at Virginia Commonwealth University (VCU) in 2008 and 2009 was the first time I truly understood how individual effort could either propel or sink a collective mission.

You see, rowing was a very different sport when compared to others that framed my awareness and early experiences of teamwork. As a baseball player, you have a specific role in any given day, a single contributor offensively. Your defense is the real test of trust among your teammates. As a swimmer, each individual race had its potential to turn the tides of a given swim meet, with points awarded to the school of that swimmer in 1st, 2nd, and 3rd place finishes. Relay races were that true test of teamwork and trust, however.

But in rowing, every stroke, across 5,000 meters of open water, can affect the success and efficiency of the entire boat. In rowing, timing is everything. A common misconception is that strength wins races. In reality, coordination of that timing, consistency of the stroke, alignment of your pace, wins races.

When a rower is off pace and sliding up too quickly in their seat, it "checks" the boat, the effect of a 200-pound adult moving too quickly in the opposite direction of their teammates, out of sync, diminishing progress. One rower pulling too hard has the effect of ripping through the water as opposed to catching the water in a smooth and controlled manner. The races are a result of training and communication. If the timing isn't right or if communication breaks down, the boat can struggle to execute turns, to execute power strokes to gain ground on the competition, or to pace as a group.

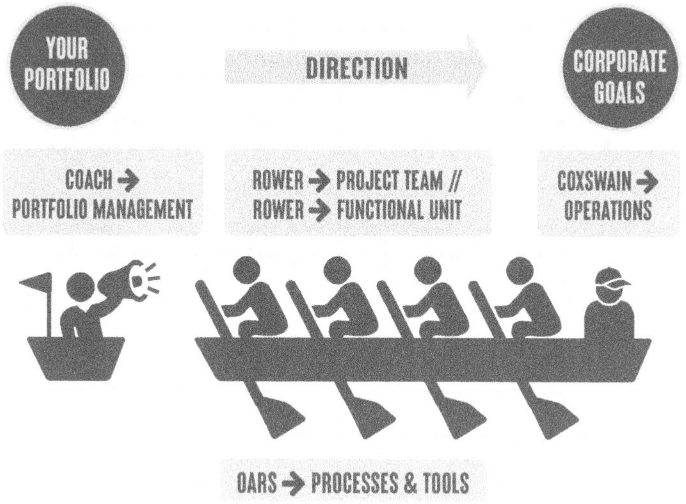

A crew team that achieves success through communication, decision-making, unity, and shared mission represents the goals and responsibilities of Portfolio Operations.

This visual of synchronized and smooth movement, shared visibility, and relentless forward motion perfectly captures the mission of Portfolio Operations in a growing biopharma organization. The real picture of so many biopharma companies, though, is a group of talented people rowing at different times or even different directions. Progress is halted by it, even if people are working their hardest to make things happen.

Yet, the intricate dance of Portfolio Operations often encounters missteps when challenges arise. Common hurdles include inadequate visibility across projects, the inability to adapt rapidly to new data, and the complexity of managing various stakeholder expectations.

Visibility into a project may not seem challenging, especially when you have a project or program manager in the role to corral the various moving pieces. But what happens when there are multiple projects, with no guidance on "how" management of it should be recorded? A project timeline may have missing tasks and milestones, critical to executing already approved goals. Perhaps dates have not been maintained, and now there are people new to the team, struggling to understand where the team is and what progress has been made.

New research data appears and tells a different story than what was anticipated. Now, the team has to collate strategies and perspectives to develop a new narrative, present it to leadership, and hopefully maintain their target timeline for a Development Candidate (DC), the point at which the enabling of Investigational New Drug (IND) experimentation begins. It's a point that requires deeper regulatory expertise and certified Good Laboratory Practice (GLP) experimentation conditions. And it's a much larger point of resource consumption and risk that moves a developed asset into living systems.

At this point, you're juggling the stakeholder expectations of leadership, often with more than one viewpoint, and functional leads whose members are part of your team, in part reporting to the team. You may find that internal support functions—like lab management, procurement, legal, and finance—also have expectations. Let us not forget the added pressure of partner expectations on the communication and strategic direction of the project, just to name a few.

When these issues manifest, they can slowly erode the effectiveness of your Portfolio Operations. Indications of trouble might involve frequent project delays, misalignment between and among departments, communication blunders with partners, or just an overwhelming sense of chaos during meetings. These are warning flags that demand attention. Have you ever left a meeting, venting with a close team member about something that just happened during the meeting? That's what we're talking about here.

Address these concerns by adopting a structured framework designed to streamline operations. This framework should consider the people of your crew—the teammates and key stakeholders. The most expensive oars will not support a winning team if the team does not know how to use them.

Integrating advanced digital solutions and promoting a culture of transparency will serve to empower your team to address issues more proactively, but only if they are adequately trained and upskilled to take advantage of advanced systems. Those requirements not only enhance your agility and resilience but also position your organization to effectively navigate the ever-evolving biopharma landscape.

WHAT IS PORTFOLIO OPERATIONS?

It's always important to pin down exactly what you're talking about when you say Portfolio Operations, especially since language varies so much from one organization to another.

There are many overlapping terms in the project/program/portfolio space, but let's define our terms to start on the same page:

- **Portfolio Management**: Choosing the right programs—selection, prioritization, and alignment with corporate strategy.
- **Portfolio Operations**: Ensuring those programs are executed effectively—managing timelines, resource allocation, governance, and visibility.

Those terms are not specific to biopharma by any means. They exist in other companies that maintain various assets. Some assets are more complex to develop than others. In this case, the assets are compounds, therapeutics, and medical devices—essentially, products.

Alternatively, the assets could be a portfolio of companies within a larger holding company that provides resources and additional support, or a business with a portfolio of projects they support. Here, we're talking about services. Portfolio management is setting the right course. Portfolio Operations entail rowing the boat.

In biopharma, Portfolio Operations is a core function which is often overlooked early on, that becomes mission-critical as companies scale. Early work activities typically require a faster work pace, with a goal to quickly determine whether an idea is of enough value to the organization to continue, or whether the cost/return projections are slowly diminishing. If you're spending tens of millions on a project, you want to find out quickly whether it's still worth it. There are other projects, active and pending, that are also in play and could use resources.

For example, an early goal in the lifecycle of any biopharma company is to develop quickly and achieve standard milestones that will support additional funding rounds, in search of your first active product. Move cheaply and quickly initially, and as the data matures that provides a clearer picture for how to get there, move at a more controlled pace to match critical decision points.

Early-stage companies tend to move quickly with the growth of internal personnel driving the progress. Personnel can become heavy in more technical fields like scientists, while other more supportive functions are built up afterward. Early-stage companies can sometimes "figure it out" as they go, but at a certain point, the lack of structure catches up (and it does so quickly). How will you control operational variability when your headcount will explode in a year?

Picture the following scenario. At this point you have a team of five with technical expertise, being managed by one of the team members with the highest experience or domain expertise. After a few months go by, leadership starts asking for updates—requests that were not previously mentioned.

The lead scientist now spends two to three weeks trying to work through experiments that are in flight, while developing an update, probably in a slide deck, that is nearly 100% manually composed. How confident can leadership be that there are no gaps or risks in the project? In many cases, it becomes "show and tell." In other words, "look at how much we have done." Nine months in, no one has even looked at the goals of their work for the year.

We mistake completed work for progress. But without context and perspective, it's just that—completed work, and nothing more.

One thing I've learned from building a business, working so closely with different organizations at all levels, and connecting with my network, is that a bootstrapped company and a venture-backed company can operate very differently in the early days.

A bootstrapped business has a focus of operating sustainably. Usually these would be run very similarly to the personal finance models of the founders. They would essentially run the business the same way they manage their own finances, because the risk of failure is too high (family, home, jobs).

A venture-backed firm, which is catapulted to its potential through large financial support, has the key goal of reaching specific milestones that will eventually roll up into an answer to the question "how long will it take to get our investment return?" The difference between the two could explain why Portfolio Operations may seem like a "nice to have," not necessary early on.

So, what you experience is this growth. From 20 to 40 to a 100+ employee company. Things at the company are starting to move. Strategies, partnerships, portfolios all start to grow, at the same time. So many decisions must be made in such a short span of time. There are a million and one ways that the next 24 months can go depending on those decisions and how well an organization can execute them. If we can agree on that trajectory, I think we can agree that developing Portfolio Operations strategy early on is key to giving your organization its best chance of success. How are you going to operate this one giant experiment? And how will it adjust when it grows?

Yet, another silent progress killer lurks. Growing without an operations strategy enables silos to exist in your organization. And as you continue to grow, the silos become more evident. New functions begin to show up, new leadership, new teams—many with their own interpretation or agenda of how things should be done. New groups are empowered to make their own decisions and use their own chosen tools and software, driven by their personal experiences. At this point the lines of communication begin to change. The resolution that leadership originally had, now begins to fizzle out. Snags and bumps take longer to get through. The last 12 months of personnel and function growth reveal struggles to catch up to legacy functions that just "knew how things work." Problems will find you when you have fragmentation in Portfolio Operations.

Science becomes siloed. Timelines slip. Budgets become an educated guess. Vendors overpromise and underdeliver. The result? Leadership lacks the insights they need to make fast, informed decisions. It doesn't matter how groundbreaking the science is. Without structure, progress stalls.

But what exactly are the signs of these operational pitfalls? You might notice extended timelines where projects seem to be constantly stretched well beyond their initial deadlines. Missed handoffs can happen, something as simple as a missed communication from a teammate, discovering you could have started the next task weeks ago. Team members could seem stressed and frustrated consistently, not looking forward to the next project. There's often an unsettling ambiguity during reviews, since people may not be clear on what each vendor is doing and by what deadline. I have been a part of teams where it was not uncommon to hear, "I'm not even sure what they're doing" as we walked out of a team meeting.

These friction points in Portfolio Operations can occur because of numerous issues. It might come down to your decision-making processes, when teams feel as though there's no way to prioritize projects effectively. Instead, multiple projects may limp along well beyond their intended deadlines, at all times. Employees get overwhelmed and tired of feeling the lack of moving toward a clear finish line. If you want to see what a real culture killer looks like, build silos.

If you spot operational silos or issues with leadership teams failing to see and use real-time data to make decisions or pivots, your observation is a call to action.

Recognizing these issues is only half the battle. You also need a framework to address them. That's where strategic planning comes into play. What you need is a comprehensive portfolio strategy. Consider not only the "what" you will decide to pursue for the business—disease, indication, service offerings, for example—but also the "how." Recognize that at some point, as the organization grows, so will the complexity of answering key questions that play a role in decision-making. It's the key that unlocks the next level of results for your team because in revisiting it, you align scientific endeavors with business objectives.

Use stakeholder engagement to determine the minimum information or data that must be available to answer operational questions. Deciding what work you aim to do is usually first, and where we're most likely to stop. A comprehensive strategy can answer these questions:

- What data will each function working in the portfolio provide? What about supporting functions?
- What is the output of that work?
- What systems or technology will they use for that output?
- Who are the stakeholders for that data?
- What data would inform on the resources consumed relative to the work? How much? How long? How many people? How far did it go?
- What constraints can impact any of the above, such as regulations or physical space?
- What will you most likely need to outsource?
- How will you manage it?

All of it.

A real portfolio management strategy has a level of complexity with it. It's not merely about managing individual projects, but about overseeing them in a way that they converge toward greater institutional goals.

Consider technology integration as a pivotal part of this framework. The use of digital tracking and analytics provides transparency and facilitates swift, data-driven decisions. This facet includes technical software like LIMS or ELNs, and the software that manages your legal contracts for vendor work. These systems tend to be positioned to manage transactions, specific output from the end of a task.

Outline the technology your processes demand to produce your work. From the technology to perform specific experiments to the technology that manages the pace of projects and cash burn. Consider the limitations of that technology to report and connect to other functions.

Rarely do technical systems freely allow for collaboration. But that data is usually the context needed to connect technical operations to business operations. However, many systems are not necessarily built for forecasting or planning. They are merely a point of entry and recording of a task being executed with results. Whether you are entering a new experiment or logging and maintaining clinical site contracts, those measures are related to work on a particular project, probably with specific dates, likely to exist relative to a milestone on a timeline. They are key to progressing an asset in the portfolio, and indirectly or directly impact decision-making. If data isn't related, why are you recording it?

There's a good chance you're tracking things individually already, but that's not enough when you need open communication with an entire team. With open communication, you will not only identify risk more quickly, your ability to respond to it proactively also increases. Thus, you will be paving a path to transparency and excellence.

COMMON PITFALLS IN BIOPHARMA PORTFOLIO EXECUTION

In so much of my work across early- and mid-stage biopharma companies, a pattern emerges. While it might not be immediately obvious that they are portfolio issues, there are some sure signs that some problems may be blocking progress in your organization. Here are some of the most frequent and costly problems that fall under the Portfolio Operations umbrella:

- Delayed decision-making due to lack of project governance checkpoints.
  You don't exactly know when you need to make decisions or what you need from teams to make them.
- Disconnected or duplicate project-tracking systems with no common clarity on the actual project status.
  Everyone records their own work, their own way. Whose is most accurate?

- Siloed functional groups without shared visibility.
  You actually don't know the progress of your team members on the project. And you're next in line, waiting for the handoff.
- Inconsistent vendor management practices and budgeting.
  Who has managed their expenses? What spend is upcoming?
- Resource imbalances across teams.
  Your project stalls because there isn't enough in-house support and no budget to outsource.
- Manual data reporting, prone to errors and delays.
  "Which project is this again?" "Wait, that graph says 72 micrograms, but the last slide said 92. Which is it?"
- Poor handoffs, inconsistent execution, and low or slow knowledge transfer.
  Without knowing the "when," you struggle to plan your work as it could come to you, "any day now."

These problems show up as missed deadlines, unclear ownership, budget overruns, and high turnover. And it feels even worse. It can feel like a struggle to gain momentum with the team and clarity from leadership. The longer the problems persist, the more expensive they become to fix. And the harder it is to get buy-in from the team when they are exhausted with lack of change and increasing burdens. You can expect to find some cynics in the next "verbal commitment" from leadership.

So, how can biopharma companies and other complex industries effectively tackle these challenges?

It's essential to establish a strong operational foundation that addresses these pain points and drives efficiency.

It starts with knowing what is expected from the leadership of your organization and who can make decisions.

First, consider integrating a robust governance framework. Who can make decisions for the program or project? What are the boundaries of those decisions? When will you need to make certain decisions? By implementing clear checkpoints and workflows, decision-making becomes more streamlined and reduces delays. This confluence ensures that everyone is aligned and informed, enabling quicker responses to market demands. Your team will thank you. They now have a target to align with the expectations.

Harmonize Your Systems

Equally important is the harmonization of project-tracking systems. Your goal in selecting a system and processes for tracking your progress should be to find one that can expand, is flexible, and has the potential to connect the other pillars of the Biopharma Nexus Model. Interoperability creates a seamless flow of information, enhancing collaboration across teams. Complex projects require an equally capable system or systems. And those systems will require guidance, input, and ownership from the workforce.

In this process, be careful not to overlook the need for breaking down silos. Silos are one of the biggest problems across many departments and even entire biopharma organizations, and the problem only gets worse as time goes on without intervention.

A silo can become rigid over time, hung up on the differences of our contributions and without enough focus on what unites our contributions to a greater cause. Too many employees focused on "their project" or "their department" makes it impossible to create a truly collaborative environment.

This pattern may require a mindset shift, from an individual contributor to a critical piece of the entire system that is the organization. Encouraging cross-departmental visibility and communication fosters a collaborative culture. This shared insight helps in identifying resource imbalances early, promoting prompt corrective actions. It helps communicate unexpected changes to the project plan.

Manage External Work Well

To add to that foundational work of breaking down silos, implementing standardized vendor management and budgeting practices is crucial. External partners become key players in the quest to the next blockbuster product. These specialized vendors can also quickly be responsible for bursting budgets or extending timelines. Vendor management should have its own set of internal guardrails and expectations, even in early-stage companies. The limitations reduce both costs and the operational risk, ensuring that you have a team all rowing at the same time and in the same direction.

Technology Will Change Work

Growing up in the 1980s and 1990s, I experienced that technology boom firsthand. The advancement in communications from rotary phones to push buttons, corded to cordless, home phone to personal cell phones. The move from hardwired to Bluetooth and Wi-Fi. The internet boom. And into the dawn of Artificial Intelligence. The technology boom has been an accelerant to innovation, an accelerant to ideas, and an accelerant to action.

Technology advancement outpaces our ability to absorb new ways of performing work. Let's consider the classical technology adoption curve or bell curve. It divides the adoption of technology into four populations, often referenced in new product strategies. Early Adopters, Early Majority, Late Majority, and Laggards. In a normal distribution of randomly selected people from a population, you can expect everyone to fall into one of these categories. Each person has their own interests and needs, their own level of interest toward any new technology, and their own timeline for diving into something new.

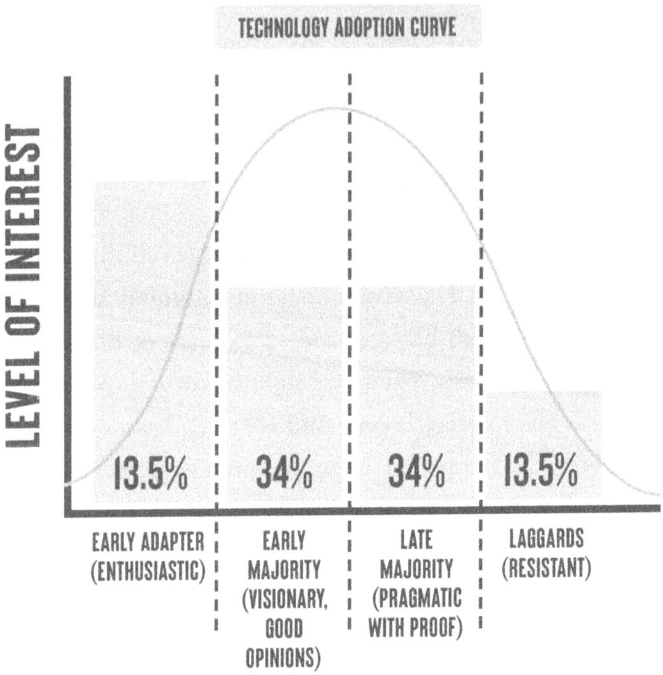

Depiction of the Technology Adoption Curve, presented as a classical normal distribution. With each Adopter Category representing a subpopulation of people.

You can expect to see something similar when you introduce new technologies to your team or organization.

The same can also be said of the pace of scientific innovation. What was once a paper-bound physical lab notebook with restrictions on leaving the workplace with it has become a digital log of our work and accessible through our internet. Finance reports that were once typed up on typewriters and saved in file cabinets can now be accessed via the company server. What we define as work will continue to change as technology advances. Complex industries demand it.

The systems you use today may not look the same in five years. The same could be said about the direction of the company. Flexibility is key.

Once you've aligned the expectations, these crucial base elements for improving Portfolio Operations, it's time to think about how you collect, analyze, and use data.

One way to think about it is to align the data output of your processes. The creativity comes in developing a solution to how your data is linked and how your people work. Ask yourself, "how will information and data flow through the teams and projects?" Leveraging existing systems and potential upgrades can provide advanced capabilities and elevate decision-making.

Starting with automation of data reporting is a vital step, significantly minimizing the potential for errors and delays. Find ways to automate team notifications of key dates from a project timeline. Or automate monthly reports to keep key leaders updated on progress.

By leveraging technology, teams can focus on analysis and strategic actions rather than manual data entry. When you introduce automations for the purpose of supporting the day-to-day through connecting and communicating all forms of data, you will find that the conversations begin to change.

Stakeholders can quickly access data and context, bringing everyone to a level playing field and advancing conversations. Updates become less interesting, and strategy becomes purposeful.

Knowledge Is Power

Lastly, but arguably the most critical, is enhancing the quality of handoffs and knowledge transfer through better documentation and clearer processes, leading to consistent execution. In one case, a new employee is part of a new role where there is no prior knowledge, in other cases they are a back-filled role or part of an existing team. Without sources of truth, procedures, or historical documentation, knowledge begins to fade and onboarding new talent requires months.

Knowledge transference not only preserves valuable institutional knowledge but also bolsters the company's ability to adapt to change. Imagine a world where a new hire can hit the ground running. A world where they can actually move through the requirements of their new position as well as understand what they have to do and whom they have to interact with. It's time to make that a reality, not wishful thinking.

Take Innovations Biotech, for example.

CASE STUDY: INNOVATIONS BIOTECH—WHEN IDEALS OUTRUN INFRASTRUCTURE

Innovations was a promising biopharma start-up formed from a merger between two early-stage companies. The scientific potential was strong. Leadership put forth a strategy that would make the most conservative investors buy in. But operationally, the organization was no more aligned than your holiday lights balled up in the attic.

They had nearly two dozen projects running simultaneously but lacked a unified system to track progress. Some projects were deep into various phases that were being conceptualized while other projects were moving through development. There were various tools being used, some for software and hardware development, a few project management tools, digital storage solutions, and workflow development tools. Their challenges were less about the tools and more about the lack of a source of truth—the lack of guidance for how teams were expected to interact and report within the available tools.

The organizational structure was equally strained. Designed purposely as a flat organization, managers had up to 25 direct reports. Leadership promoted autonomy and self-management, but without clear SOPs or onboarding, teams were left confused and unsupported.

Take the perspective from your own experiences of how your organization is structured. The majority of the people reading this book have probably experienced a hierarchy structure—a CEO, who has four or five VPs and each of those have another 5-10 senior managers and directors, each managing multiple entry-level roles. Drawn out, it looks much like a pyramid.

The issue we come across when considering a "flat" organization is that the large majority of employees who will eventually be hired are not familiar with working with heaps of autonomy and a low amount of direct management. It is a strategy that ignores the culture shock and provides no guidance of how decisions are made or what decisions can be made. Leaving teams to their own devices to manage and to progress projects is a surefire way to build disjointed operations. In this case, major infrastructure investments were made without proper go/no-go decision checkpoints.

The result? Burnout, confusion, and millions spent with no clear framework for evaluating success. We found uncertainty among teams on what the finish line was for their part of development. And an inability to review previous decisions or plans as each phase of development was handled by a different team with different requirements and expectations on the data they were collecting and the phase goals. Worse still, when key risks were raised and solutions proposed, leadership failed to act.

This inaction is common in the industry. Companies acknowledge the pain but delay the remedy, often until issues become existential. What we often find is that with the disconnected data, there is an inherent inability to develop proper insights. Leadership "hears" of issues and challenges, but setting aside any potential biases or urgency elevation related to the proximity of the team and the issues, leadership will typically refrain from making any major decisions to this end because there is no data to support the insights. The risks come across as inflated emotional responses rather than markers of a poor strategy and execution.

BUILDING AN EFFECTIVE PORTFOLIO OPERATIONS FRAMEWORK

To counter those issues, companies need an operations framework rooted in five pillars:

1. **Unified Project Tracking**: Select and integrate tools that support collaboration and transparency across all functions.
2. **Governance**: Create decision gates tied to meaningful data, not gut instinct, enabling the portfolio to progress with clarity.
3. **Resource Management**: Ensure balanced workloads and visibility into team capacity, leveraging digital resources, and balancing project-level cash flows.
4. **Vendor Oversight**: Centralize contracts, budgets, and capacity planning.
5. **Operational Cadence**: Standardize reporting and communication rhythms.

Each pillar must be built with the company's stage and growth trajectory in mind. For example, in a 40-person R&D shop, "governance" might mean one standing leadership review each month. A 400-person clinical organization with partnerships might include tiered review boards, defined escalation paths, and structured portfolio committee decision-making.

Portfolio Operations is not a one-size-fits-all function. It is a living system that must form and scale with the business and its people.

CASE STUDY: DISCOVERY THERAPEUTICS—TURNING CHAOS INTO CLARITY

This engagement provided opportunities to grow my empathy for the organization and its responsibilities to its employees and stakeholders. The initial role was to fill a program manager gap that was the result of growth and new partnerships. In any new role, I've learned to lead with humility and ignorance. I don't know anything about how this company runs that isn't public. When I do learn how the company runs, I'll learn who the players are and how I can support them in removing friction. The naivety we push ourselves to experience when landing at a new organization can humble us, correct our biases, and open opportunities to enhance our work and to those around you.

When I joined Discovery Therapeutics, my first move was to understand the tools that were being used to manage their portfolio of projects. This initial effort would be for a single project among a sea of active and planned projects and programs. Let's consider the expectations for this role and how its data was organized.

This role required timeline management, budget management, vendor management, team and roster management, program progress and goals management, and updates and insights from research & development. For a moment, let's break down this role's data, how they were originally managed, and discuss where systems stalled. These challenges can emerge when there is rapid growth in people and systems, and no reflection.

The timeline for a project was the "source" data for projections on activities and financial burn. They included estimates of key executive milestones at their highest level, with more granularity on dates and durations for expected activity. This data had just recently been moved into a software system that I just happened to be expert in. By this point it had been over 10 years and more than 10,000 builds to manage work in biopharma.

There was just one problem: Their timeline didn't cover much, just executive milestones. There was no guidance for the team to utilize a highly detailed timeline software, so the majority resorted to manual edits to a slideshow. Static timelines were presented and modified, on an as-needed basis. Comparisons across the portfolio took hours upon hours of manual manipulation to existing slides to provide a worthwhile view. A challenge due to presentation software lacking predecessor linkages—a connected timeline for when one task moves, so do the tasks that depend on the completion of the former.

Picture going through a presentation with timelines. Each project has different colors, font sizes, naming conventions, and scale—some in months, others by quarter. The variation in formatting of similar data, like these timeline presentations, inevitably creates friction in moving from the review of one project to the next.

So, as our eyes struggle to reorient to what the conversation is about—the project name, phase of development, progress, risks, unique needs and challenges—we miss opportunities for insight because we are now distracted by format differences, which our brains automatically recognize, as we navigate the portfolio. There was no single source of truth, only frustration.

When I landed this role, it wasn't my first interaction with the group. We had a two-way interview to understand whether this position made sense mutually for us to engage. When I discovered that the team lead did not lean strongly toward any of the systems in use, we left the door open for what an improved solution could look like in the end.

In the project manager role, I was given the freedom to manage the project how I chose, so long as I executed the work. So, my role as a project manager further turned into another opportunity to elevate the work of the people around me—consistency, ease of use, reportability, better insights, better conversations.

Beta Test the Value

I started by piloting a solution on my project. Everything went into it—goals, team rosters, meeting notes, timelines. This wasn't my first rodeo. These were common work products for project managers. They were also areas of friction for leadership and decision-making. Designed with the organization in mind, we linked live views to provide decision-makers with the data and insights. Multiple stakeholder views were possible from the source information, connecting cross-functional teams to what matters most to them.

We linked portfolio views across internal spaces so that anyone, from any function, at any time, could access current, accurate data. We designed the start of a system that would grow organically at the pace the organization demands.

Making Solutions Sticky

Now, designing and building a system isn't all that's required. Adoption of this new way of working is also a living part of the organization. These sorts of initiatives are not successful unless you have great relationships in the organization. Change requires empathy and patience. You will have early adopters who are more excited to jump in than you are. You will also have laggards who seem nearly impossible to get on board. But there's this massive percentage of people in the middle. Maybe they feel they don't have the time or feel a bit burned out and that learning a new system is just another task to delay them. They also recognize, though, that change has to happen.

To connect with those in the middle, empathy needs to jump in. In moments where we may fall into highlighting the system features as the strong point of our introduction to those involved, we must not neglect to learn the issues in their work. We must learn of their experienced friction on daily work, and develop a relationship baked in empathy. When people feel seen, they are less likely to fight against change, knowing there is support to follow through. These changes are less about the systems themselves and more about the connectedness of what we do every day.

Becoming a champion for the system will drive the right people to also take on a new system, become fully engaged, and become a champion themselves advocating for the value of this new connected system. This effect is why you do not silo operational change. Advocates across functions are stronger than a single team of advocates.

Moment of 'Ah ha!'

Once the system revealed itself to stakeholders through day-to-day activities, regular trainings, and frequent leadership communications, the perceived value came into focus. As adoption grew, that value was realized.

Our quarterly reviews became efficient, focused, and even asynchronous. Portfolio reporting took minutes, not days. And we moved from being reactive to proactive. We have to also recognize that leadership will continue to have questions, only this time they're deeper, more informed. Those ad hoc reports were constructed in near seconds, truly expediting insights for decision-making.

At this level of change, people start to notice. Even the biggest critic can show curiosity, paving the way to the required stickiness of change management. Eventually, other teams wanted in. Functions that had been isolated began asking how to adopt the same model. The silos were falling, and the organization was becoming a living system.

The transformation wasn't about the tool. It was about the mindset. We didn't just bring visibility. We brought accountability, curiosity, agility, and resilience to the operations.

SCALING UP: FROM PROJECTS TO PORTFOLIO STRATEGY

Portfolio Operations is not just glorified project management. It requires an entrepreneurial mindset. Each project is a small business with a strategy, budget, staff, and timeline. Multiply that by 20, and you need scalable systems and a team that thinks like operators, not just trackers.

It also means understanding trade-offs. In a resource-limited environment, your best opportunity to succeed starts with prioritization based on data and scenario planning. Operations leaders must constantly ask: Are we investing in the right programs? Are our teams balanced? Are vendors delivering what they promised? How much cash runway do we have? Are we leveraging our resources? True Portfolio Operations lives at the intersection of science, strategy, and execution.

At Oncology Therapeutics, we learned the imperatives firsthand.

CASE STUDY: ONCOLOGY THERAPEUTICS—BUILDING SYSTEMS FROM THE BENCH

My first industry role was as a lab manager. It was a small lab, no more than 10 people. The only consistency was in a few typical lab assay SOPs. The operations had no standardization. Procurement was done on sticky notes. Mere hand-written scribbles with no vendor information or requirements. There was no inventory system, no tracking on spend, quantity, or frequency. So, I built one from scratch.

My attention to detail became apparent to leadership when a simple task in support of an upcoming New Drug Application (NDA) filing revealed discrepancies across research reports that were previously submitted, years prior, when filing the IND application to begin clinical trials. Fortunately, these discrepancies were found to be immaterial to the foundational claims represented in the data. However, it is to be expected that discrepancies could have delayed the review.

That work led to a promotion into program planning, working closely with clinical operations, where I found clinical trial timelines being tracked by two owners in a system with limited access across trial managers. This separation stuck out to me as odd, especially given there were six other ongoing projects. But the position was a career transition. What did I know? Well, I had the facts. Multiple projects with multiple project managers that were responsible for their project's timeline and executing it on budget. Sometimes easier said than done.

To be grossly simplistic, a clinical trial has a start-up phase, a maintenance phase, and a shut-down phase. Each with its own sets of milestones, challenges, and hurdles to clear. What I learned in a span of just a few days was that start-up for a clinical trial is extremely complicated. Starting a big one could require coordination of hundreds of people across organizations, roles, domains, and languages. Looking at the portfolio, we expected hundreds of patients across hundreds of sites over multiple studies, with no real-time visibility into the progress.

My first task was to support and manage the timelines for a large global Phase III clinical trial. Those initial solutions I spoke of didn't come with the structure I speak about in this book—they were built selfishly.

If I had to manage a timeline, I wanted a way to connect other people who were responsible for carrying out the activities. I wanted to understand the task-level nuances of major cross-functional deliverables. I wanted to see enough into the future that we didn't feel blindsided when change happened.

Also evident to me was that team discussions moved slowly because of real-time navigation lags during meetings. Everyone, on their laptop, was digging through their system, preparing for the next question or discussion topic.

The situation presented an opportunity to remove the friction. Upon discovering a new work-management system to pilot our Phase III, I presented the solution to my new manager, a C-level executive. "If we move on this, you have to know more about this system than the rest of the organization, including IT."

They gave me an opportunity to lead a transformation. With it, we integrated clinical ops, legal, finance, chemical manufacturing and control (CMC), and medical affairs into a shared real-time system, displayed internally for maintained alignment. Development governance became fast and focused. Site timelines were visible to everyone, and decisions were made with confidence. Future projections now had data to support planning.

All because we invested in visibility and structure.

And the benefit wasn't just execution. It was an influence. By delivering reliable data, we gained trust from executives, partners, and regulatory bodies. This change enabled the organization to respond to unpredictable friction. That's the hidden superpower of Portfolio Operations: it gives the business confidence.

CLOSING THE GAPS: WHERE MANY BIOPHARMA COMPANIES FALL SHORT

Far too many organizations pour resources into project intake and launch, but neglect the day-to-day scaffolding of execution. Portfolio Operations gets treated like an administrative reporting function when it should be a strategic lever. Poor communication, inefficient tools, and forgotten project transitions cost real money and erode trust and morale.

Project transitions are especially critical failure points. Many teams excel at onboarding new projects but have no plan for how to manage knowledge transfer across milestones, phase handoffs, or staff turnover. When institutional knowledge lives in someone's head, or worse, is buried in an email inbox, operational resilience suffers and the risk to your strategy begins to creep.

It's not enough to hit major milestones. Teams must learn to optimize the "in-between", because most of the risk (and value) is created between project kickoff and final approval.

> The organizations that succeed are those that understand the race isn't won at the start or finish line—it's won in the thousand strokes in between.

DEEP DIVE CASE STUDY #1: INNOVATIONS BIOTECH

WHEN PORTFOLIO OPERATIONS CLASHES WITH OPERATIONAL CHALLENGES

Portfolio Operations challenges can face biopharma companies of all ages and sizes, but can be especially prominent for start-ups scaling quickly. In the case of one stealth-stage start-up I worked with, a combination of foundational and operational challenges highlight just how difficult it can be for start-ups ready to enter the quick growth stage while starting to integrate emerging technologies.

The company faced five challenges that held back their ability to grow and capitalize on this opportunity. Many of these challenges will be familiar to other biopharma leaders, too. Which challenges below do you identify with?

CHALLENGE #1: ORGANIZATIONAL AND STRUCTURAL MISALIGNMENT

At the time I worked with Innovations, the company was less than two years old with a headcount of around 50 people. The company's leaders knew that growth to 100 people was a must in the near future.

Despite this growth trajectory, the company maintained an overly flat structure: single managers overseeing as many as 25 direct reports. This structure led to unclear accountability, a lack of formal project leadership, and confusion about roles. The leadership vision was for everyone to act as their own project manager, yet there was no infrastructure or guidance to support that.

You can't embolden people to lead successfully without giving them any kind of guidance or infrastructure to do it well.

Challenge #2: Tool and System Fragmentation

Innovations operated with multiple unintegrated systems—multiple project management systems, software and hardware development, folder systems on internal servers and personal computers—without clear guidance on which platform was the source of truth for projects or documentation, nor the ownership therein. This mix resulted in duplicative efforts, inconsistent naming conventions, and siloed knowledge. The merged organizations, two companies that came together six months before engagement, had not standardized systems or workflows, creating deep confusion.

Reaching out to stakeholders early in our engagement only led to a ping-pong of where the source of truth was and who owned it. This back and forth only created confusion and missed the chance to have one source of truth and project status. Eventually this created duplicate work, since everyone followed their own system for documenting updates.

Challenge #3: Lack of Portfolio Visibility and Project Governance

Project timelines were not actively managed, with tools like the software development system being misused for tasks it wasn't designed for (e.g., tracking R&D project milestones instead of software builds). The company had over 20 active projects, yet no overarching portfolio view or way to track dependencies and progress. The workflow was fractured. Ownership of projects would pass through multiple hands and systems without continuity or historical tracking.

There was also a dangerous lack of governance checkpoints. Multimillion dollar infrastructure decisions (e.g., purchasing robotics, building out lab space) were being made without clear go/no-go decision frameworks or risk-mitigation strategies.

There was no real governance in place to flag a stop before they spent another $10 million.

Challenge #4: Cultural Ideals Without Operational Backing

Leadership promoted ideals like "one consciousness" and empowered autonomy, expecting team members to self-organize and lead. But without processes, SOPs, or onboarding support to enable it, dysfunction followed. Expectations were mismatched with capabilities and infrastructure, especially in a scientific environment where time and focus are dominated by experiments.

Can any five people in a room somehow figure it out? And hit expectations? Unlikely.

Challenge #5: Missed Opportunity for Change

Despite surfacing these issues through an early discovery process, the company ultimately chose not to move forward with implementation. Feedback suggested that leadership didn't fully understand the scope or value of the recommendations. This decision reflected a broader industry challenge: Many biopharma companies recognize pain points but delay action, often until the issues become existential.

The good news is that no matter how many of these challenges you're dealing with or have struggled with in the past (yes, even if all five resonate), there are things you can do to fix current projects and implement the Biopharma Nexus Model to streamline and scale effectively.

As we've seen in the previous case studies, operational challenges in portfolio execution are rarely isolated incidents—they reflect broader patterns of misalignment, system fragmentation, and underdeveloped governance. To further illustrate how these dynamics manifest beyond the biopharma industry, the next deep dive shifts our focus to a real-world scenario drawn from higher education.

While anonymized for confidentiality, this example highlights strikingly similar themes of resource misallocation, operational inefficiencies, and missed opportunities for structural change. The parallels will underscore just how universal—and solvable—these challenges can be when approached through the lens of systems thinking.

DEEP DIVE CASE STUDY #2: BOSTON ACADEMIA

WHEN SCIENCE MEETS SYSTEMS: A CASE STUDY FROM HIGHER ED

Early in my career, I joined a research lab affiliated with a major Boston medical center. Officially, I was brought on as a laboratory technician. In reality, I stepped into something much more complex—a lab in transition, trying to scale research operations without the infrastructure to support it.

The lab had just secured new funding—a start-up grant from the university, and an NIH research grant. That funding meant we had the green light to grow, to bring in graduate students, launch experiments, acquire resources, and expand the research portfolio. But like many academic labs, we were missing the operational scaffolding needed to support that expansion.

Academic roles were somewhat informal, documentation was spotty, and budget tracking was almost nonexistent. Looking back, my early research career was surrounded by well-funded work. It came with a better prepared infrastructure.

I hadn't realized how broad a career in conducting scientific research could look—vastly different experiences, different guardrails, different structure, different decision tree, different rules, different purposes, and different needs. And in other ways, the difference tracks well with what challenges we see, in that academia trains the next biopharma manager or executive.

Misallocated Funds and the $50,000 Surprise

There were different processes for purchasing standard consumables, and for purchasing equipment. Also, we had partnerships and access through the NIH as grant recipients, which had a separate process for procurement. Nothing was documented.

One of the first red flags came from a simple spreadsheet. I'd been trained to place all lab orders using a single account number. After a few months, I realized that no one had mentioned the second, much larger grant we were supposed to be drawing from. I asked my PI if we should be splitting expenses between the start-up fund and the grant. His response: "Of course. We should've been doing that all along."

That's when I discovered we had overspent the start-up fund by about ***$50,000***. Thankfully, the overage hadn't hit our actual invoices yet—a by-product of vendor invoicing delays at the time. But this misstep exposed a larger issue: The lab had no process for reconciling spending with grant allocations. We were flying blind financially, relying on incomplete data and outdated habits.

The Inventory Iceberg

Finance wasn't our only problem. Our inventory system was just as fragile. We had multiple versions of high-cost reagents like antibodies that would cost hundreds, stored in fridges and freezers, many of which had failed experiments, were incompatible, or were simply unused and frozen to ice. No one had documented which had worked, which hadn't, or why.

This deficiency led to waste—not just in money but in time. Researchers reordered items we already had because they didn't trust what was on the shelf. In one cleanup effort, we tossed out thousands of dollars' worth of unusable materials. It became clear that our inventory wasn't an asset. It was a liability.

Operational Lessons from a Shared Space

Another challenge: working in shared space. Our lab was one of three within a single quad of a floor. We had overlapping resources: equipment, bench space, safety oversight, but little to no coordination. Everyone operated independently, which worked fine until it didn't. Experiments would get delayed because someone else planned a full day's worth of specialized experiments on their most common resource. Time-sensitive materials would arrive before a station was available. We were constantly bumping into each other, figuratively and literally.

Even in this situation with limited resources, there are opportunities to improve, and opportunities to build culture, accountability, and resilience. So, I started implementing lightweight coordination systems: weekly checks on equipment availability, group messages to release lab space, inventory notices when stock was low. These weren't high-tech solutions, but they worked. Over time, the lab started to function less like three separate rooms and more like one coherent research operation.

A Scientist's Mindset, an Operator's Lens

What made this experience transformative was realizing just how deeply operations affect outcomes, even in a research environment. Scientists are trained to develop questions, design experiments, analyze data, and publish findings. But few are trained to manage inventory, track budgets, or build systems that scale. Yet without those systems, research stalls. Money is wasted. Effort is wasted. People burn out. All you feel is friction because everything is difficult, and nothing is changing.

I didn't walk into that job with all the answers. But I did bring a mindset of curiosity and problem-solving. I talked to our grant administrator regularly. I rewrote the inventory spreadsheet system because that's what we had access to, while also leveraging the system beyond the initial use, tapping into more advanced capabilities. I built financial-tracking models that linked project spending with research timelines. And eventually, I helped the lab get clear enough on its operations to publish its findings, apply for larger grants, and continue growing.

The Broader Implications in Research Operations

If there's one lesson I took from my time there, it's this: Research Operations are still operations. Whether you're managing experiments, projects, or people, the same rules apply. You need visibility. You need accountability. And you need systems that support, not stifle, your goals.

Academic labs often treat operations as an afterthought. But if you want research to thrive, you can't afford to leave operational excellence up to chance. What starts as a misplaced purchase or a disorganized freezer ends up as lost time, burned-out teams, and missed opportunities. The science might be cutting-edge, but if the systems don't keep up, the whole structure starts to wobble.

That lab taught me how to think like an operator in a scientist's world. And it laid the foundation for everything I've done since.

FINAL THOUGHTS: OPERATIONAL EXCELLENCE AS A COMPETITIVE ADVANTAGE

Portfolio Operations may not be glamorous, but it's the backbone of scalable innovation in biopharma. It turns hope into plans and plans into products.

It also builds culture. When operations run well, teams trust the process, communicate clearly, and stay focused. When operations fail, chaos becomes the norm, progress slows, and people leave.

Operational excellence carves sightlines into your most vulnerable areas, exposing your risk, providing an opportunity to become a responsive organization. From start to finish, moving a new product or asset across development and into the hands of patients is a notoriously unpredictable journey, one that often finds its way into, and is owned by, multiple organizations with their own strategies, goals, and plans.

Whether you're supporting one program or 50, building a strong operational core allows your team to move in sync, adapt quickly, and make informed decisions. Just like a crew boat cutting through the water—controlled, fast, and with a shared direction.

Operational excellence is not an afterthought. It is your edge. A mindset.

With aligned goals in place, the next step is to create systems and structures that empower teams to move from intention to execution.

Chapter 3 Takeaways

- Progress depends on synchronized efforts, not just individual strength.
- Portfolio Operations turns strategic goals into coordinated execution.
- Everyone should know how their work ladders up to company priorities.
- Transparency in goal setting encourages accountability and trust.
- Simplicity in goals encourages focus and execution.
- Technology adoption without stakeholder alignment creates fragmentation.
- Goals are not just metrics—they're commitments to impact.

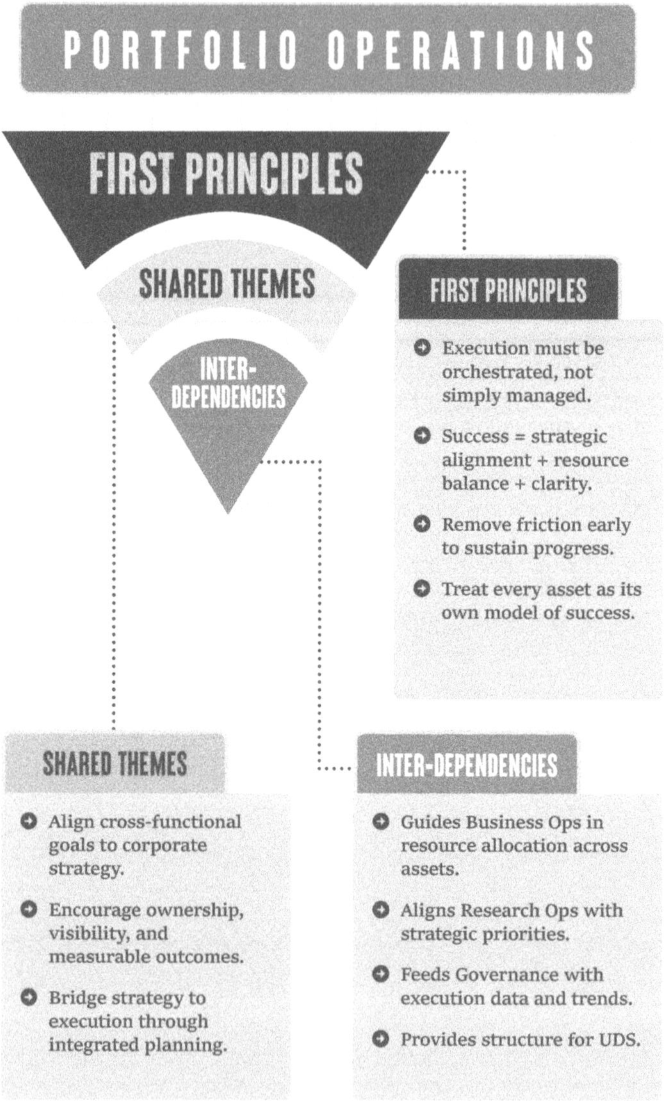

The Portfolio Operations Nexus Wedge its first principles, shared themes, and interdependencies to the Biopharma Nexus.

CHAPTER 4

BUSINESS OPERATIONS—THE INFRASTRUCTURE OF SUSTAINABLE GROWTH

INTRODUCTION: SCALING WHAT MATTERS

BUSINESS OPERATIONS COMPRISES the foundation upon which an organization grows—not a luxury function for well-established organizations, but a critical enabler of scale, clarity, and resilience. Especially in high-complexity industries like biopharma, where execution must align with regulation, shareholders, innovation, and cross-functional collaboration, Business Operations becomes the center of gravity.

Yet, for many early-stage companies, operations is deprioritized in favor of scientific or commercial acceleration. This imbalance creates friction: Teams are hired before systems are ready, vendors are onboarded without contracts, and timelines are managed on spreadsheets instead of on platforms.

The Biopharma Nexus Model recognizes that operational maturity is not a switch—it's a spectrum. It grows as companies grow. It connects strategic intent with tactical execution, empowering people with the right tools, governance, and clarity to succeed. This chapter unpacks the role of Business Operations through a lens shaped by my real-world experience, from lab benches and budgets to executive coaching and enterprise-level diagnostics.

What emerges is a vision of Business Operations as the connective tissue of a high-functioning organization. Done well, it aligns purpose with performance. Ignored, it creates invisible bottlenecks that become the very risk that the company sought to mitigate.

What Business Operations Actually Does

Business Operations, at its core, is the infrastructure that powers execution. It encompasses the systems, processes, and people that turn strategy into progress. Unlike a siloed department, operations is inherently cross-functional—it touches finance, legal, HR, IT, compliance, research, and more. It ensures that contracts are processed, vendors are onboarded, budgets are tracked, and tools are adopted.

My experience building Sigma Lab Consulting exemplifies this approach. As a founder, I wore every hat: legal, finance, procurement, and HR. In doing so, I discovered just how interconnected these functions are. Side-quests throughout my career revealed glimpses of this connection that only recently became visible. Each decision in one domain impacts others. Approving a new hire affects budgets. Onboarding a vendor requires contracts and budget compliance. The introducing of software triggers training and data governance. Business Operations is the system that keeps these dependencies from becoming your greatest liabilities.

It also plays a cultural role. When well-resourced, it reduces burnout, increases efficiency, and helps employees feel like they are part of a coordinated whole. In fast-growing environments, it is not just about adding structure. It's about enabling scale.

Diagnosing the Problem—Symptoms of Operational Breakdown

Operational breakdown often manifests as subtle friction before it explodes into obvious dysfunction. Symptoms may include delays in processing contracts, budget surprises, unclear vendor timelines, or teams duplicating work. Leadership may not recognize those indications as signs of a systemic problem, often attributing them instead to "growing pains." But these recurring issues stem from operational gaps that could be solved with proactive systems.

For example, while managing a Phase III timeline, I identified major challenges in tracking site-level clinical timelines across over 175 sites. Each department—legal, finance, clinical—used different naming conventions and categories. This setup created confusion in reporting, delayed cross-functional decisions, and introduced regulatory risk. The solution was not more staff, but more alignment. I implemented standardized naming, dashboards, and a process playbook to align these functions, enabling their data to connect and deliver insights that were once educated guesses.

These are not isolated cases. Across biopharma, when operations are neglected, even the best science gets stuck. Business Operations provides the visibility, structure, and accountability that help organizations function smoothly.

Why These Problems Persist—The Start-Up Trap

Many start-ups romanticize chaos. Scrappy, do-it-yourself execution becomes a cultural badge of honor. Early team members wear multiple hats, improvising systems and processes on the fly. This attitude can create early traction, but it is not sustainable. As teams grow and the complexity of the work expands, the cracks in these improvised systems begin to show. Systems don't scale. Knowledge isn't transferred. Critical work is lost in chat threads and spreadsheets.

I saw this pattern repeatedly, but it was especially visible at an academic research medical school. Despite having secured top-level NIH funding, lab teams operated in financial silos. Budgeting was reactive. Oversight was informal. And most problem-solving relied on individual heroics rather than team coordination. That mode is a hallmark of the start-up trap: Success depends on a few experienced people compensating for the lack of structure.

In such environments, growth doesn't resolve the chaos—it amplifies chaos. Business Operations must evolve in parallel with the team. That function needs to be introduced early and scaled proportionally. Without it, burnout spikes, turnover increases, and execution slows. Business Operations may not be flashy, but it is the function that allows scale to happen without collapse.

The People-Process-Technology (PPT) Triad

The origins date back to the 1960s from the "Diamond Model," a framework to manage change in an organization. It later became a more simplified and popularized version as the PPT "golden triangle" by Bruce Schneier in the 1990s, a specialist in computer security and privacy. It eventually became a business mantra. People, process, and technology are the three pillars of change management execution. They're interdependent—when one shifts, the others must adapt.[14] In the Biopharma Nexus, Business Operations is the function that aligns and calibrates all three.

My work in R&D project management offers another strong example. When I was brought into a new organization as their first project manager hired to help standardize project workflows, I didn't just introduce software. My approach focused on facilitating conversations between scientists, operations leaders, and IT. They aligned on what workflows were needed, what cross-functional views would show, and how decisions would be made. The result was more than a new tech rollout. In reality, it was a cultural change rooted in accountability and innovation.

14 "People, Process, Technology (PPT) Framework: Pros and Cons," *Prosci* (blog), last modified August 19, 2025, https://www.prosci.com/blog/people-process-technology.

The mistake many companies make is thinking that technology alone solves operational problems. An even bigger mistake is thinking that IT is the only group responsible to manage it. But technology amplifies what's already there. If your process is broken, software will exacerbate, then expose, the pain points faster. If your people aren't trained, no platform will save you. Business Operations ensures that systems are adopted in a way that supports both performance and morale. It doesn't just install tools—it teaches people how to use them, supports adoption, ensures alignment, and builds upskilling and confidence of the organization.

LEGAL AND FINANCE—SILENT PARTNERS IN EXECUTION

Business Operations often functions behind the scenes, but its success depends heavily on how well it integrates key functions like legal and finance. These departments are not just back-office necessities. They are also strategic enablers. They govern how money moves, how risk is managed, and how partnerships are made possible.

My work with a pre-commercial R&D organization highlighted how disconnected vendor onboarding processes had become, a key process for a growing organization with limited headcount. What was originally presented as a five-step process was really a series of 25 steps between identifying a need and signing a contract. Each one introduced friction, especially when legal and finance weren't aligned on which signature was required first to enable the other to sign a contract. I streamlined this process by aligning stakeholders on the true process of what was actually happening at the organization and related pain points.

I introduced documentation standards, decision trees, and accountability for turnaround times. It wasn't just about reducing time-to-contract. I reduced confusion, increased compliance through follow-up training, and rebuilt trust between process owners and key process stakeholders.

Business Operations sits between strategic goals and the systems needed to support them. By aligning legal, finance, and operations workflows, companies gain speed, reduce risk, and create clearer pathways to execution.

Technology—Choosing Tools That Fit the System

Every biopharma company uses dozens of digital tools across functions. The challenge is not acquiring tools, it's integrating them. Too often, a new leader brings in a platform they've used before, without considering cross-functional compatibility. Soon, three departments are tracking the same projects in three different systems.

At an early R&D stage company, I encountered this problem head-on. Their projects were at the intersection of artificial intelligence, machine learning, and foundational lab bench science. An incredibly complex portfolio.

Teams were using two separate project management systems, one specific to software and hardware development, along with a virtual document-storage system to manage overlapping parts of the same portfolio. Data was duplicated, decisions were missed, and leadership couldn't see the full picture.

At the time, they were lacking a project management skill set and mindset at the organization.

Leadership had relinquished decisions to individuals on how to manage the work, enabling silos to begin construction. To this point, about a year into operations, leadership had not experienced a full portfolio view of the progress and status for their 20+ ongoing projects. With this client, I conducted a systems audit and discovered discrepancies in the understanding of which systems should be used and what the requirements were for each system.

There had not been subject matter experts (SMEs) for the systems of use, widening the gap in the "how" of managing the activities and projects. This situation led to a proposition to align leadership on language and nomenclature, with the purpose of aligning the newly merged leadership and developing a sound data architecture, guiding the road map to a unified solution.

But not everyone will hop on board. In this industry that demands a high level of intelligence and deep vertical knowledge, ego can sometimes get in the way of innovation.

A major challenge I've experienced with leaders through the years is the prevalence of "group think," a term to describe a feature of brainstorming when someone initially expresses an idea and everyone in the conversation sticks to that idea and continues to iterate. However, when ideas are pondered through divergent thinking, those methods push the boundaries of what is possible.[15]

---

15 An exercise that takes different formats in having individuals ponder problems, ideas, or solutions in isolation, broadening perspectives as opposed to coming from a single thought line.

Stakeholders are usually positioned to think about key problems or possible solutions in isolation. This separation provides for wider perspectives, generating a pool of ideas that can be discussed, rather than building solutions on a single outspoken individual.

Perhaps the value wasn't clear when presented. Perhaps the organization was not prepared to make the kinds of changes in leadership that could position teams for success. The root causes of the challenges began to reveal themselves. But a major factor required for success in building and rebuilding efficient and effective practices, reducing operational risk, and aligning the strategy to action, is leadership humility.

Business Operations ensures that technology adoption is more than just installation. It aligns tools with strategy, trains teams, and drives governance. Technology should never be a silo. It should be an enabler of transparency, clarity, and speed.

Building Internal Talent—Training and Ownership

Companies often overlook the importance of operational training. Tools are introduced, but onboarding is *ad hoc*. Documentation is scarce. Knowledge becomes tribal. And incomplete system processes are riddled with workarounds. This lack of formal training leads to rework, wasted time, frustration, and uneven performance across highly paid individuals.

Training is a foundational operational responsibility. At Sigma Lab Consulting, we have built playbooks, templates, and walk-throughs for every system process we were involved in. This experience revealed how much confidence is tied to competence. When people are trained, they ask better questions, offer improvements, and feel empowered to drive effective change and lead discussions.

When building internal talent try starting with the following:

- Determine the critical systems for the organization's work, or your team's work. What systems do you have in order to do the work you were hired to do?
- Initiate a program to train multiple employees to become SMEs and functional systems owners. This strategy develops internal champions of key systems at your organization or with your team.
- Schedule and provide regular training on the foundations of the systems you are using. Refreshers will enable a baseline systems knowledge across your organization.
- Provide case demonstrations to reach additional users and adopters of the new systems.

Business Operations should include continuous development. It should offer regular tech refreshers, process updates, and feedback loops. Employees shouldn't just use systems. Instead, they should own the systems. And when they do, operations become a source of innovation, not resistance.

Implementing the Biopharma Nexus Model in Business Ops

The Biopharma Nexus Model introduces the Nexus Transformation, a three-part framework:

1. Detect & Diagnose
2. Contain & Simplify
3. Fortify & Adopt

Each step is driven by operational insight and execution.

At some point, you've probably asked yourself, "why are we doing it this way?" As you reflect on the reason and consider possible challenges, you will quickly find that the issues are in layers. And those layers begin to pile up. Real fast.

To make meaningful change—change that sticks, change that drives culture into working smartly and freeing up time for reflection—the key is to understanding pain points, and where operations are most at risk of harming the organization.

Detect & Diagnose begins with great questions, something I never really paid much attention to. "What was the event that led to the issue surfacing?" instead of "Who did it?"

Naively, I figured that creating conversation was enough to prompt an understanding of an issue or challenge. My interest in questioning had little to do with consulting or problem-solving and everything to do with the notion that great questions can spark breakthrough ideas. The book *A More Beautiful Question* by Warren Berger takes you through a process of asking Why, What If, and How for innovative questioning.

For me, to be successful with diagnosing a real problem (the source, that is), I needed to first understand the questions I would be asking to discover the root challenge. There is an immense amount of humility required when diagnosing a problem. In doing so, you position yourself for a focused diagnosis, reducing any internal biases.

Berger writes that "if What If is about imagining and How is about doing, the initial Why stage has to do with seeing and understanding."[16] His perspective hints to a subsequent Why stage.

The stronger your diagnosis, the higher the likelihood for your solutions to stick.

The second requirement for asking great Why questions is to challenge what we "see" or "understand." When faced with a problem, we rarely have a full picture. That's one place where solutions fall flat. You solve the wrong problem by asking the wrong questions. True insight begins with taking a step back and asking why.

Instead of asking "who gave the authority?" try asking "do we have a process for decision-making?"

---

16 Warren Berger, *A More Beautiful Question: The Power of Inquiry to Spark Breakthrough Ideas* (Bloomsbury USA, 2014), [Page 75].

A good way to become unpopular in a business meeting is to ask, "Why are we doing this?" (even though the question may be entirely justified). That was me. The same person who had a question at the end of class when the professor asked, "Any questions?"

Solving problems can go unnoticed in some organizations. If things feel frictionless, it's because people have been diagnosing and solving problems. You may be mandated by leadership to "just get it done," which implies driving right to a solution—a trap that many fall into.

Stepping back from "doing" is only one side. We have to step back from "knowing" what the problem is as well. When we hear, "build me a dashboard" from leadership, and respond by doing just that, pretending that we know the problem we're solving, we risk doing things again. And again.

"Why do you need a dashboard?" Go ahead. Ask the question. And continue to ask questions until you truly see and understand the problem. Only then can you develop the right solution to answer the right question.

Why are these problems happening? Why do people care? Why did leadership get involved? Develop that understanding more deeply than your peers. At a small biopharma company that exploited fungi for producing natural genetic molecules, similar to how penicillin was discovered, I ran cross-functional interviews to map every process in R&D from the initial experiment design and culturing to the purification of a naturally produced targeted molecule. It was a full process that demanded roughly 80% of the company employee resources at some point along the journey.

Stepping back from what you know creates a picture, one that many at the organization may never see. The picture shows the true network of the operations of your most critical resource. This practice reveals things about your operations.

Patterns emerged—bottlenecks in function handoffs, processes with no clear ending, unclear platform usage or data format, for example. But it also presents opportunities to remove roadblocks and simplify your processes as well as to address unclear ownership, overlapping platforms, and gaps in reporting mechanisms. And it presents opportunities to eliminate risk from your operations.

When executed well, stakeholder questioning provides the context for which challenges are front of mind.

- how challenges impact operations
- who the responsible cogs are
- understanding the current state
- envisioning the future state

A great Detect & Diagnose result is one that has a raw, unbiased view of the current state and its pain points, and paints future goals in outcomes, not software features.

Contain & Simplify, the next stage, alleviates key bottlenecks and paints a path to remove duplication. It looks for the most effective use of resources. Of course, there are times that the constraints to our problem's resolution may prevent reducing some of the burden or challenges, a common hurdle in heavily regulated industries, but don't abandon the effort toward improvement.

Use an operations map, which paints a picture of how work is done and the connecting nodes across functions. With it, you can see any excessive overlap or areas lacking attention. Apply those discoveries. Imagine a complex discovery process to develop a natural medicine, for example. There may be areas to simplify operations such as how and where you culture your organisms—human cells, animal, fungi, or bacteria—despite constraints on the conditions based on FDA regulations for natural medicines.

Don't stop at simplifying a process. Make it simpler for people to know what to do, simpler to understand navigating the process. Make it simpler to get trained or ask questions. Simplifying clarifies roles, aligns language, and reduces process drag. At Discovery Therapeutics, I was able to cut onboarding steps by half through documentation and decision gates.

Fortify & Adopt is the work that secures your investment in making change. It is where change becomes culture. It's not enough to fix a system. No. You must also teach, reinforce, and govern improvement. It requires the energy to build excitement, empathy to meet people where they are, stamina to continue building awareness, and understanding adopter challenges.

Areas to consider are

- company awareness campaigns
- internal SME office hours for support

- regular, available training commensurate with staff attrition rates
- available process documentation and recordings
- individual internal champions to expand reach for key changes

Enablement and support for internal adoption must remain consistent for a more organic path to culture change. Through it, people will begin solving other problems and challenges when they feel there is follow-through and support from the organization. When teams know what "good" looks like, how it feels, and how to repeat it, Business Operations becomes a multiplier to your organization's capabilities and strengths.

WHAT BUSINESS OPERATIONS ENABLES

When Business Operations functions well, everything speeds up. Project launches are faster. Budgets align with timelines. Vendor approvals happen in weeks, not months. Morale improves because people trust the system. Teamwork improves because there is alignment. Conversations evolve, even from the unlikeliest of sources.

I recall one moment at Discovery Therapeutics when a newly onboarded team member showed a series of reports and dashboards they had built independently, a month after joining. It was a tool that visualized partner timelines, budget forecasts, and milestone progress. It wasn't assigned work. It was *enabled* work. It was another sign that my system had taken root.

Business Operations, done right, builds clarity. It reduces guesswork. It creates space for people to focus on their core strengths. And it scales. What once required 10 emails becomes one form. What once depended on one expert becomes institutional knowledge. That's the power of integrated Business Operations.

How to Think About Business Operations

For most biopharma companies, Business Operations covers a number of key functions and business units. Some are more universal, like human resources and facilities. Others, however, may be more specific to an industry. For example, some industries might have an AI department.

There can also be some nuanced differences in how groups decide to organize themselves, such as tall or flat. Within this Biopharma Nexus Model, I call out legal and finance functions due to the large role they play in accessing external resources to move the company forward.

At its core, Business Operations function to support and enable the success of the organization. The people, the processes, and technology behind Business Operations play a critical role in supporting the overall company mission.

People, Process, and Technology

This concept is nothing new. This PPT framework is most recognizable from the business and IT space for managing changes in process and technology. I propose that it should be taken one step further, making this trio an active component of biopharma business operations as opposed to a single initiative. Then it will become a living, breathing asset to a healthy organization.

People are the driving force behind every portfolio. The program managers, technicians, scientists, decision-makers, partner vendors, and infrastructure support are the people who execute the minutiae of applying strategy behind every portfolio. Every strategy, concept, program, project, goal, and task depends on the talent within the organization to move forward. To support their success, organizations invest in technology that enables and enhances skills, standardizes processes, and captures the data needed to track progress. As the portfolio expands, the complexity increases—so too does the importance of choosing the right individuals to manage and support that portfolio.

Those three components—people, process, and technology—must grow in harmony. When one evolves, the others must adapt. The role of Business Operations is to ensure this alignment, continuously nurturing the relationship between workforce, systems, and strategy. This pillar has a key responsibility of Business Operations, which is to ensure that staff receive appropriate training and support for the tools required in their daily work.

Surprisingly, many organizations overlook regular or available training for essential technologies. From human resources platforms to enterprise project management systems, nearly every aspect of modern organizational work is digitally captured. This digital footprint ties together the "what," "who," and "why" behind key initiatives, forming foundational tools for data-driven decision-making.

Why Technology Friction Happens in Biopharma

When an organization is in its early stages, IT typically sets up foundational systems such as email, internet, phones, shared drives, and the standard office software. That work creates a baseline. As the organization grows, however, new technology needs to emerge. IT may play various roles in addressing these needs, sometimes leading the evaluation and implementation of new tools, and other times acting as support while functional leaders source their own software.

This delegation of ownership to individual departments can result in siloed software use, inconsistent training, and fragmented institutional knowledge. Left unaddressed, a common outcome is that different departments will use similar tools in different ways—or worse, choose incompatible systems that hinder collaboration and severely diminish the strength of your insights. Don't be surprised if you start to see multiple nodes of expertise in your company's most critical software. These gaps can slow internal progress, and even worse, crush morale.

Consider the onboarding of a Clinical Operations group preparing for the upcoming Phase I clinical trial. This team may need several systems for managing patient data, project timelines, regulatory approvals and guidance, vendor management, site-level legal contracts and budgets, drug supply and dispensation, adverse-event reporting, and Key Opinion Leader (KOL) engagement. Each area can require its own vendor or software solution.

In most cases, the responsibility for selecting and integrating these tools falls on the functional lead—often a VP or director—who must handle selection, implementation, onboarding, training, and maintenance. The initial focus is usually on getting the tool running quickly and in training immediate users. With tight timelines and financial stakes high, these leaders are often left to "figure it out" rather than execute against a coordinated technology roadmap.

FRAGMENTATION IN FUNCTIONAL GROWTH

The five key functions in a clinical trial—clinical operations, data management, pharmacovigilance, chemistry manufacturing and control (CMC), and medical affairs—often evolve at different times and rates. Rarely are they established simultaneously or with consistent oversight of their software stack. Each incoming leader typically selects tools that meet the needs of their domain, often without input from adjacent functions.

This autonomy may seem beneficial, but it creates serious downstream consequences. Even if all systems use standard identifiers for trials, sites, or patients, the way data is recorded and displayed may vary. The effect is difficulty in producing integrated, high-level views of portfolio performance. As a result, program updates for leadership become time-consuming and error-prone.

Where data management requires compliant password-protected systems that contain patient information, including enrollment data, project timelines are managed by a different team in a different software only available to that function. Financial projections would most often find their way into an excel spreadsheet. Combined, this data can provide the backbone to understand the enrollment rate (the pace at which patients are onboarded into the study), financial burn (how quickly funding is exhausted as a function of the enrollment pace), and study timing (actuals and projections for completing enrollment, maintenance, study closure, and planned data lock). Separately, these data sources can answer standard questions: When are we projecting the completion of enrollment? What is the average time a patient is in the study? What are we spending on our projects each month? Together, the data generated from these three sources creates context to the current and future state of the clinical trial. Cross-functional insights grant clarity and confidence in decision-making.

Yet, we need to know *how* the data is being compiled. Ask yourself: Do you know what your colleagues in another department do each day and how they track their work? In most growing organizations, the answer is "no." This lack of cross-functional awareness leads to inefficiencies, duplicated efforts, and knowledge silos. Even small differences in naming conventions or data structure can create major obstacles to synthesizing insights across a portfolio.

Ownership, Training, and the Cost of Inconsistency

When software is adopted, the process owner is responsible for ensuring that (1) team members are trained, (2) onboarding occurs smoothly, and (3) the system is actively maintained. It has been my experience that this responsibility is left to the IT Department, which is more often focused on the company infrastructure and security. Unfortunately, that arrangement often results in uneven adoption and performance across the organization. Some teams and team members become power users while others barely understand the basics.

Take Finance, for example. Not uncommon is the use of a common spreadsheet software to generate projections and financial scenario planning. A majority of the population more than likely has created a financial sheet or two completely by hand. A smaller group would use advanced features like macros, which help by automating a set of actions that are repeatable with a single click. The smaller group has the advantage. Gaps can appear in any function and create imbalance in the internal talent pool.

Gaps are especially evident in project management tools. Some project managers may thrive, using automation and dashboards to stay ahead. Others may struggle, forced into manual processes simply because they were never trained on the platform's full capabilities. Over time, these discrepancies affect the health of projects. Inconsistent practices stall progress and frustrate team members. Others find themselves picking up the slack or being chosen to lead every initiative, reducing confidence in those less capable.

Business Operations can help solve this predicament. Regular training and walk-throughs should be available—not just pointing users to generic vendor presentation slides, but offering internal sessions that reflect how the software is used within the organization. These sessions help illuminate capabilities that might otherwise be missed and provide context for the data being collected.

Technology should not be treated as a fixed expense but as an evolving capability that grows with your team. Without recurring systems training and process standardization, organizations risk developing underskilled staff and variable output quality. If technology isn't well supported, projects become dependent on manual work-arounds. Decision-makers are left with fragmented data that lacks the necessary context for portfolio-wide insights.

Building a Culture of Enablement for Thriving Business Operations

It is not enough to offer "office hours" or *ad hoc* support. A strategic approach to upskilling the workforce is essential, especially for Level 1 stakeholders—the ground-level individuals executing day-to-day tasks. Functional ownership of tools should come with accountability for training and documentation. Each software product should have an internal SME who leads onboarding and regular training.

Enable your teams to introduce and own the technology that powers the portfolio. Support them by providing funding for training and resources that can further the development of teams and users.

Let's return to the example of a project management tool owned by the PMO. If only a few team members truly understand how to use the system, project performance will vary. Without standardized training, operational inefficiencies will persist. Over time, Business Operations can bridge this gap by introducing consistent systems training that equips users with both technical knowledge and an understanding of how the tool aligns with organizational goals. Galvanizing your teams to level up their skills and to elevate their work removes bottlenecks and evolves the company's maturity.

Legal and Finance: Unsung Pillars of Operations

Among the most critical functions in biopharma are Legal and Finance. These teams support operational continuity and risk-mitigation. Legal protects the organization through contractual and regulatory compliance. Finance manages budgeting, cash flow, and strategic allocation of funds. Both functions often serve as final gatekeepers for releasing funds to external vendors.

When setting up a new vendor, technical consultant, strategic consultant, CROs, or other service providers such as contract laboratories and regulatory submissions support, the Legal team is a required stakeholder to ensure compliance and obligations. The Finance team is a required stakeholder to ensure that the work is budgeted with the required approvals to release funds.

The collaboration of both departments is central to the vendor engagement lifecycle. In many organizations, every dollar spent externally requires a contract. These agreements vary from simple vendor portal terms to individually negotiated contracts. Smaller organizations often rely on one-off contracts, which can delay onboarding due to negotiation complexity.

Those variables create a delicate dance between Legal, Finance, and project teams. Multiple stakeholders, differing data sources, and software systems complicate the process. Yet, their alignment is essential to bringing vendors onboard quickly and keeping programs on track. These support teams are often overlooked in operational planning, but the data they generate (spanning both financial and legal realms) is critical to informed decision-making.

The Broader Challenge in Biopharma

The global market for contract research organizations (CROs) and vendors serving biopharma is worth billions annually. Organizations rely on these external partners for flexibility, expertise, and scale. However, the process of engaging them—through contracts, onboarding, and systems integration—takes time and coordination.

I've experienced delays firsthand in the start of a new project at a new organization. We had the go-ahead from leadership. The client sponsor was excited to get started and have their team engaged. There was only one problem: This was a non-budgeted contract (as are many consulting engagements) and demanded a separate workflow as a new vendor. The proceeding weeks were a series of back-and-forth emails with the legal team, while fielding queries from the client sponsor regarding the progress of the contract and start date. Our eventual start date was pushed back by more than a month. This lag occurred despite the first outreach three months prior. Lack of foresight of the details involved halted progress.

Functional teams must balance the urgency of project timelines with the diligence required to onboard external support correctly. When Business Operations is involved early, these transitions can be smoother. When it is left out, operational inefficiencies can ripple across the portfolio, and improvement and mitigations are delayed.

Business Operations is not just about overseeing tools or enforcing compliance. It is about building a connected, well-trained workforce that knows how to execute. The systems used across an organization are more than software—they are the infrastructure of progress. When training is regular, ownership is clear, communication flows between functions, and the organization can move with clarity and speed.

By supporting people, aligning technology, and enabling integration across teams, Business Operations becomes the engine that drives execution at scale.

THE HUMAN IMPACT—MORALE, GROWTH, AND MEANING

Operations isn't just about systems. It's about people. When business operations run smoothly, employees feel supported. They know how to succeed. They don't waste time duplicating efforts or working low value tasks.

I have seen team morale change drastically after operational improvements. At Natural Medicines, teams that once dreaded weekly reporting exercises began using dashboards proactively during team calls. Why? Because the data reflected their actual progress, was a live feed, and helped them plan ahead. It wasn't about compliance. It was about clarity.

When people are empowered, they take initiative. They bring solutions. They stay longer. They cultivate excellence. Business Operations fosters a sense of order that translates into a culture of accountability and respect. That benefit is its hidden power.

Final Thoughts: Business Operations Is a Strategic Imperative

Business Operations is often invisible when it works, but impossible to ignore when it breaks. It's what connects strategy to execution, enables cross-functional clarity, and gives teams the tools to do their best work.

The Biopharma Nexus Model recognizes that operational systems must grow alongside scientific progress. In every company I have worked with (from labs to venture-backed platforms), the difference between stress and stability usually stemmed from operations.

Business Operations is not an afterthought. It is what I call the "thought line." And when companies invest in it early, they build not just capacity, but confidence, culture, and scale.

Chapter 4 Takeaways

- Business Operations is the backbone for enabling strategic action.
- "Scrappy chaos" is not sustainable.
- Cracks will amplify as the company grows.
- People, Process, and Technology must evolve together.
- Technology alone cannot fix a broken system.
- Overlapping systems without alignment create inefficiency.
- Investing in Business Operations enables speed and clarity.

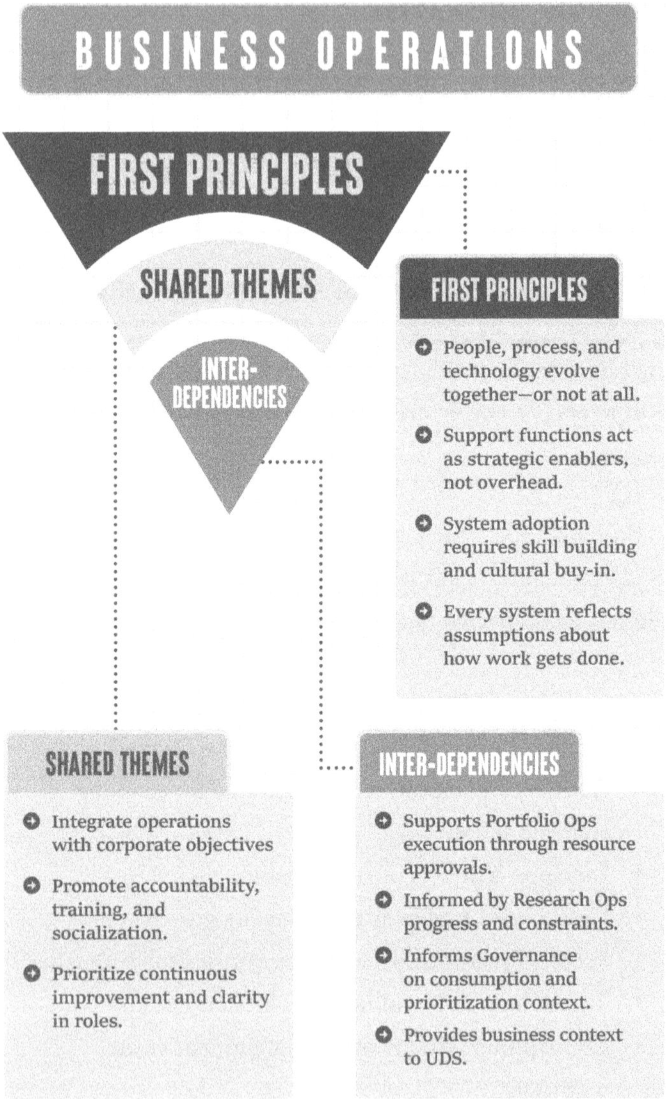

The Business Operations Nexus Wedge its first principles, shared themes, and interdependencies to the Biopharma Nexus.

CHAPTER 5

GOVERNANCE—THE OVERSIGHT FRAMEWORK

INTRODUCTION: PROVIDING STRUCTURE FOR LONG-TERM SUCCESS

IN THE INTRICATE world of biopharma, where every decision can carry multimillion-dollar consequences and life-altering outcomes, governance acts as both compass and guardrail. Governance isn't just about who gets to make the final decision. It's the system through which oversight, accountability, and strategy converge. It helps organizations scale with intention, maintain integrity across silos, and ensure that innovation doesn't outpace infrastructure.

Governance, done right, is not a bottleneck. It is the framework that enables fluid decision-making, strengthens communication, and enhances organizational agility. But when it's disconnected from operations, or treated like a paper exercise, it can create confusion, waste time, and slow progress.

This chapter explores the role that governance plays in the biopharma lifecycle, how to structure effective oversight, the dangers of governance bloat, and how high-functioning organizations make governance work for them, and not against them.

DEFINING GOVERNANCE

The term governance itself can be hard to define. It's a loose term that organizations use in different ways. So, let's get on the same page with what governance really means.

Start by thinking of it in this way: In your organization, who makes the big calls? How are you organized? Clear decision authority in organizations is not just helpful to streamlining things in this industry—it's essential. But too many biopharma companies operate haphazardly in this way. Either there are "too many cooks in the kitchen" or governance is a loose term referring to an outdated, mostly ignored charter.

Governance is the process by which a company's leaders and key stakeholders organize themselves to make critical decisions on behalf of the organization that materially impact portfolio strategy, innovation strategy, funding allocation, work staff resources, and partnerships.

A governance body often includes C-level executives (e.g., CEO, COO, CFO), portfolio managers, and functional leaders across R&D, clinical, and operations. These individuals must bridge cross-functional concerns, balancing strategic vision with scientific rigor and financial realities.

Why Governance Starts with Clarity at the Top

When I think about governance, I think about clarity—specifically, clarity around who has the authority to make decisions and how those decisions get made. One example that has always stuck with me is the challenge of co-founder equity splits. I've seen a lot of people default to 50/50 splits when starting a company (of two founders). It feels fair. Equal. But that approach can create real issues down the line, particularly when it comes to leadership and decision-making.

Let me be clear: I'm not saying a 50/50 split is wrong. But it becomes problematic when it masks an unclear power structure. Who makes the final call when the team hits a disagreement? Who's responsible for prioritizing resources or setting strategic direction? Without defined roles and a clear path for breaking deadlocks, decisions stall. People get frustrated. Progress slows.

The importance of decisional clarity is why governance isn't just about boards, committees, or formal policies. It's about how we organize decisional power and responsibility from the very beginning. In companies that avoid this early conversation, governance ends up happening by accident: Decisions are made based on who speaks loudest, has the strongest title, or simply happens to be in the room. Happenstance is not sustainable, especially in high-stakes industries like biopharma.

As the Biopharma Nexus Model shows, the governance wedge plays a vital role in everything we do—from cross-functional teams and portfolio planning to compliance and culture. But it's not just a single wedge. It lives within teams, departments, and even project-level relationships. When project leaders don't know who's empowered to make what call—or worse, when no one agrees on who owns what—it leads to friction, confusion, and costly delays.

So, whether you're starting a company with a friend, managing a growing R&D team, or leading at the executive level, governance starts with clarity—clarity in roles, clarity in decision rights, and clarity in how disagreements get resolved. And while equity may be split down the middle, responsibilities almost never are. The more proactively we define governance structures—formally and informally—the better positioned we are to execute with confidence and build trust across the organization.

THE ROLE OF GOVERNANCE IN BIOPHARMA

At its core, governance answers a simple question: **How do we structure ourselves to make and support decisions?**

In a biopharma context, governance typically involves

- decision-making bodies (e.g., executive committees, program review boards)
- structured oversight for programs, research, and resource allocation
- regular milestone reviews
- risk-management planning
- strategic direction and portfolio alignment
- innovation support for systems and processes

As companies scale from early discovery into later-stage development and commercialization, governance grows in importance—and complexity.

Why Governance Exists

Good governance in biopharma typically centers around two core goals:

1. **Strategic Decision-Making**—Evaluating whether programs should proceed, pivot, or be halted based on updated data, risk profiles, or budget realities.
2. **Organizational Support**—Helping teams escalate challenges, align cross-functional priorities, and advocate for resources.

Governance bodies should not function solely as a rubber stamp or a place to deliver updates. Rather, they should provide real oversight, actively troubleshoot systemic issues, and serve as a conduit between executive leadership and ground-level operations.

Picture yourself at an organization where your leadership is known by name and rarely seen. Governance committees are the one place that you can expect to receive input from the leadership, addressing questions like "should we go with a slow-release compound or an extended release?" Each outcome is a major strategic pivot because developing medical formulations can be a costly part of drug development. The best answer requires adequate data and a decision tree or pros/cons to guide the committee with as much data and insight as possible. Such are real questions that unfortunately do not always get the time they deserve. Their importance escalates especially when the portfolio grows, yet the agenda now leaves just 12 minutes to consider a strategic shift valued at hundreds of thousands of dollars. And that's if the committee even gets to your program! Otherwise, the decision gets pushed another two weeks to the next meeting.

How Governance Connects Data, Research, Portfolio, and Operations

As with every other aspect of the Biopharma Nexus Model, governance is linked to the other pillars. It is an overarching thread that impacts multiple aspects of operations.

In practice, governance is the connective tissue between and among major operational components:

- **Data**: Data from research and clinical studies informs strategic pivots, resource allocation, and investment priorities.
- **Research**: Governance bodies help validate whether preclinical or clinical research is ready to advance.
- **Portfolio**: Governance ensures prioritization of the right projects, manages attrition, and evaluates resource trade-offs.
- **Operations**: Oversight committees can help streamline decision-making, reduce bottlenecks, and mitigate execution risk.

- **Business**: Governance often provides the final approvals for major business decisions that can cost or save precious resources.

When governance is siloed from these functions, or focused too narrowly on reporting, it loses its power to guide and correct course.

Ensuring Transparency and Accountability

Transparency is a pillar of effective governance, yet it's often one of the first things to erode as organizations scale. Early on, governance transparency is a direct feature of small businesses, related to the leadership's proximity to early employees. As the organization grows and expands, multiple functions form with employees therein. The voice of governance becomes diluted through the expanded business and management layers. This eventual transition requires appropriate attention to ensuring a communication rhythm and flow from leadership governance.

Decision-making for teams can appear to be a grey area when transparency is lacking, when a project stalls, and when waiting for that next opportunity to get a straight answer. I've experienced firsthand attending a governance meeting that ended in a blowup because a strategy was implemented that did not go through the committee itself but was approved by other leadership. Transparent governance can only happen when committee members and stakeholders adhere to open and frequent communications, which ensure the greatest insights to move the portfolio forward. Poor cross-functional alignment (particularly when stakeholders don't have clarity on who owns decisions) can create massive drag on a company's ability to move itself and its portfolio forward.

Common symptoms of ineffective governance in biopharma organizations include

- teams that are unaware of who has final authority to approve decisions
- projects that are delayed because committee feedback is unclear or contradictory
- preparation for meetings that becomes burdensome due to lack of clear expectations or multiple review cycles
- feedback from governance that is inconsistent or forgotten between reviews

To counteract those issues, governance must be explicit. Define who belongs on which committees, what authority they hold, what types of decisions they are responsible for, and how teams should prepare to engage with them.

Governance as an Enabler, Not a Bottleneck

Many governance structures become bloated over time, leading to what I hear often described as "dog and pony shows" where teams present to multiple overlapping committees, often duplicating effort.

In one organization, I witnessed the growth from two committees to six within a year, prompted by projected growth in partnerships and the projects therein. Governance charters were provided. However, they overlapped with some of the responsibilities of the legacy committees and had overlapping members. Along with their core executive leadership committee, there were additional ones for resources, research, operations, and partnerships. Whenever a partnered project was discussed, the content had to be reviewed by another subcommittee to gain a stamp of approval prior to sharing it with any partners.

What made it more interesting was that not every committee could make a formal decision, yet they were required to review a project prior to its being submitted to the executive leadership committee. In the end, the results were perpetual cycles of developing and modifying presentation content to audiences that varied no more than 20-30%. With constant work toward an update cycle that took two months to produce its final decision, such overlap is never the intention. However, it is a reality of rapid growth without reflection.

Common governance pitfalls include

- **too many overlapping committees** with unclear jurisdictions
- **poorly defined charters**, leading to confusion about who makes decisions
- **committees that don't follow through** on member responsibilities like pre-read expectations or actions
- **transactional meetings** focused on formatting or optics rather than substance

- **lack of leadership support**, where governance bodies demand updates but don't engage meaningfully

The result is that operational excellence becomes a disconnected paper exercise—boxes are checked, but no meaningful changes ensue.

True governance should *reduce* friction. It should clarify direction, streamline funding decisions, and eliminate unnecessary prep cycles by aligning around what truly matters.

Building a Governance Framework that Works

The best governance systems are simple, scalable, and grounded in real business needs. If you have one that is outdated or not really serving the purpose as I've described in this chapter, you may want to start fresh. Use the line of questioning below to get the foundation and considerations for an appropriate governance.

---

1. Scope & Authority
What is the scope? What authority would they have?

2. Decisions
What decisions do you make?

3. Stakeholder Involvement
How can members of the organization participate, and get input?

4. Leadership Commitment
How will the committee prepare?

5. Follow-Up Discipline
What happens after the meeting?

6. Balanced Attendees
Did you engage representative stakeholders in your blast radius?

7. What to Govern
Outline points of risk for a business.

a. Strategy - What problem the company solves, and how it intends to do so.
b. Funding - The money you need to do it.
c. Resources - The things and people needed to execute.
d. Delivery - Assess how well work is executed, and enables innovation.

Many more early-stage programs require different governance rhythms than do later-stage clinical trials or commercialization efforts. As such, the framework must be adaptable, not static.

Scenario Planning and Risk-Management

Governance is the last line of defense against organizational risk, and it's also the first place where plans should adapt to emerging realities.

Scenarios to consider include

- budget overruns due to geopolitical or supply chain disruptions
- program failure based on new data
- key partnerships stalling due to misaligned priorities
- layoffs or reorganizations that impact team capacity
- mergers and acquisitions that change the company structure
- leadership changes that shift lines of command

A strategy that considers the possibility of failure is a strategy that can pivot when unknown risks arise. Governance often fails to account for risk proactively. It's not enough to wait for teams to raise red flags. Governance bodies must ask hard questions about what could go wrong and how the company is preparing for it.

The Role of Governance and Innovation

Biopharma companies must strike a delicate balance: Structure is essential for accountability and compliance, but too much rigidity can kill innovation. Create the guardrails and core procedures for your teams, and have explicit expectations for the group. The flexibility comes in how those expectations are met. Governance should be part of the conversation to support and enable innovations that support its North Star.

Many biopharma governing bodies sometimes reject bold, data-backed ideas as "too visionary." Yet, they also demand innovation. This contradiction highlights the need for controlled innovation, where governance sets clear thresholds for data, but remains open to transformative thinking.

A well-designed governance model fosters innovation by

- creating space for teams to propose bold ideas without fear of rejection
- supporting iterative development and process improvement
- avoiding "checkbox excellence" by promoting collaboration over individual heroics

Innovation isn't just about what new science gets funded. It's also about how the organization evolves its operational backbone to adapt and grow.

Let's look into three examples of how governance issues can show up in an organization. While your story might be slightly different, see what common threads you can spot from these studies.

CASE STUDY 1: INNOVATIONS BIOTECH—A CULTURE OF CHAOS WITHOUT A COMMON LANGUAGE

When I first started engaging Innovations Biotech, I wasn't officially working with them yet. We spent nearly four months progressing conversations that bounced from stakeholder to stakeholder, never fully understanding who the project owner was going to be, before they decided to bring me in. From the outside, they seemed like a rocket ship—a promising biotech company with massive funding, working on highly technical, AI-driven platforms. But internally? It was like walking onto a home construction with no foreman or blueprints. Everyone was improvising and not necessarily in harmony. Everyone was "busy," things were moving fast, but I couldn't quite tell who was driving or where they were going.

Once I was embedded, it became clear: They had no Unified Data Structure—no agreed-upon language, no single source of truth. They used four or five different platforms—software management, project management, slideshows, spreadsheets, internal tools—but each one told a different version of reality. Teams were logging project timelines in multiple places, none of which matched. Someone would say, "Oh, we're two weeks ahead," but a quick look at another system said they were three months behind. And worse, people would refer me to timelines provided by vendors that hadn't been updated for weeks or months. After doing some digging, I was eventually routed back to the original timeline owner who pointed me somewhere else. It was impossible to tell what was accurate.

One of the root issues was a complete lack of governance over what was fact and what was speculation. I would discover new project records simply because a system auto-published them and notified users. I'd get email alerts saying, "Here are 20 new plans created last week," and I had no idea who made them, what stage they were in, or whether they were actionable. There were no versioning rules, no reviews—just raw, unchecked data flowing into view.

The governance model was also absent. Teams were essentially self-governing, and leadership took a hands-off approach. People were being asked to project manage themselves, even when they had no project management training. So, naturally, whoever had the loudest voice—or the most senior title—would end up driving decisions, or even worse, no decision at all, which created silos and confusion.

When we proposed our approach and confirmed a future state, the organization wasn't ready. After two months, they requested a pause on our Detect & Diagnose efforts. The company had just merged with another, and the two halves were using completely different systems, languages, and workflows. Instead of harmonizing the two, they had just let them operate independently, which meant the data coming from each side didn't align, and the downstream teams (especially those responsible for execution from both sides) were left drowning in translation work. The lack of assimilation created a large bottleneck in development, crippling any progress.

What stayed with me most was that they had *never once conducted a meeting that aligned all active projects*. Not even one. For a company with over $200 million in seed funding and plans to scale to 100 people in a year, the absence of any data strategy was both shocking and unsustainable. The beginning stage of ineffective project management was clear—inconsistency.

CASE STUDY 2: ONCOLOGY THERAPEUTICS—THE NAMING PROBLEM THAT BECAME A TRACKING CRISIS

At Oncology Therapeutics, I started out as a lab manager with no exposure to the big-picture strategy or governance issues. But things changed dramatically when I was pulled into a higher-level role reporting directly to a C-level executive after just five months. Suddenly, I had a front-row seat to how governance—or the lack thereof—was affecting real-world operations.

One of the most striking issues we faced was a lack of standard nomenclature across our clinical trials. Different departments had their own ways of referring to trial activities and recorded metadata. For example, a single clinical site might be known by its legal entity in finance, its hospital name in the operations department, and its principal investigator's name in regulatory. Those variations may sound like a small detail, but they made centralized reporting and decision-making incredibly difficult.

Team meetings, especially during study start-up, involved frequent up-and-down communications on the status of various required checkboxes to activate a clinical site as ready for trial. Some were tied to successful completion of another function's activities. Simply put, there was no real-time way to understand how close a site truly was to becoming active and enrolling patients—the next major milestone for the trial. The picture offered only arbitrary project tasks driven by guesstimates.

To fix the disconnect, I created a universal naming convention: a concatenated system that incorporated site numbers, hospital names, and PI names into a single standardized format. It allowed us to link disparate datasets and build real-time dashboards that presented a clean, unified view across the portfolio. It sounds simple now, but it was transformational. Once we could trust that "004 – MGH – Dr. Smith" meant the same thing everywhere, we could start to scale reporting and resource allocation. Cross-functional insights were possible that previously took hours to craft.

But that wasn't the only problem. We also had a massive regulatory crisis related to a pharmacovigilance inbox. A dedicated email inbox had been set up to receive adverse-event reports (AEs) from across our global trial network, but no one was checking it. It had a responsible party, but that role had been eliminated, and their responsibilities were never completely transferred. By the time we discovered the issue, there were close to 10,000 unread emails, many of which could have contained reportable safety data.

This discovery triggered a full shutdown of all our clinical trials. For two weeks, the entire company was redeployed into triage mode. I helped design a project workflow that connected teams across compliance, medical affairs, and data management. We built a process to scrape, review, and categorize every email as well as to reconcile the database to ensure all regulatory authorities had been properly notified. It was an all-hands-on-deck crisis that exposed just how dangerous a lack of data governance could be.

What emerged from this chaos was a new understanding of what data governance truly means. It's not just about building dashboards or setting naming standards. It's about ensuring that the right data gets to the right people at the right time, and that no critical information falls through the cracks. We learned the hard way, but the changes we made ensured that we never faced that kind of risk again.

CASE STUDY 3: DISCOVERY THERAPEUTICS—BRINGING ORDER TO A 25-STEP MAZE

My time at Discovery Therapeutics began with a straightforward request: "Can you help our vendor-onboarding process?" What I uncovered was anything but straightforward.

They were struggling with governance at the portfolio level, especially around how they onboarded vendors for their complex, multi-partner research projects. At first, I was handed their "process map"—it was five steps long: (1) acquire the statement of work (SOW), (2) send it for review to legal, (3) then send it for review to finance, (4) submit it into respective portals, and (5) obtain signatures. That was it.

But when I began interviewing stakeholders across legal, finance, and project teams, the real story came out. Everyone had a slightly different version of the process. Some thought legal came first, others thought finance did. I discovered that there was a procurement team, but many were unclear of their role in vendor management. Internal requirements lacked clarity, which led to slow vendor onboarding that required multiple rounds of internal communications to resolve. Some members never saw the finalized contract before it was executed. The result was a chaotic system where vendors were onboarded inconsistently, contracts sat in email limbo, and project timelines suffered.

After mapping out the current state, we ended up with a 25-step workflow. Yes, you read that right—25 steps. We had to laugh about it because it looked absurd, but every single step was real and necessary. And that was the problem. These steps were happening already, but nobody had formalized them. Nobody owned the governance of the process. By stepping back to name that process and determine each step from beginning to end, we formalized it. We also got the chance to look at it with fresh eyes and determine where we could make things easier in the future.

We worked to standardize how vendors were vetted, onboarded, and integrated into projects. We improved communications processes to align how to cascade information to functional leads, ensuring everyone was aware of incoming contracts and funding requests. It was decided not to focus on changing the process, rather to ensure that employees and functional leads all understood the steps to onboarding a new vendor and SOW. Just having visibility into who needed to sign what and when was a massive leap forward. The company also began a preferred vendor list to expedite onboarding for vetted, previously used vendors.

Beyond the mechanics of vendor onboarding, what stood out to me was how often governance bloat set in. As partnerships became more complex, so did the governance layers. Every decision required multiple rounds of internal discussion before it could be taken to an external partner. Teams were caught in a cycle of creating slide decks, gathering feedback, and reworking proposals—often without ever resolving the underlying issues.

At its best, governance can help drive clarity, speed, and alignment. But without strong data structure and operational support, it becomes a bottleneck. Discovery Therapeutics was trying to be proactive, but they needed a structured framework to back it up.

Once we provided that feature, they started to see the value of unified data, not just for vendor management but for program-level decision-making across the entire portfolio.

FINAL THOUGHTS: LESSONS FROM HIGH-FUNCTIONING ORGANIZATIONS

Across dozens of biopharma companies, a few governance lessons emerge:

- **Simplicity wins**. Over-governance stifles progress.
- **Defined scope matters**. Don't rely on memory or tribal knowledge.
- **Committee discipline.** Preparation for governance goes both ways.
- **Support beats sign-off**. Governance should advocate for improvement—not just approve it.
- **Governance needs governance**. Revisit the structure every few years. If no one has looked at the charter in three years, it's already outdated. And trust me, by that point, no one knows what's in it or why.

Governance is often seen as a burden, and as something companies tolerate rather than leverage. But the most effective organizations recognize it as their greatest tool for consistency, strategic focus, and scaling with integrity.

It's not about creating more committees or reporting layers. It's about crafting a clear, adaptable structure that supports decision-making, communication, and continuous improvement.

When done right, governance doesn't just protect the company, but also propels it forward.

Governance establishes the boundaries of progress. It enables development of people-based solutions to business problems. Complex organizations demand governance clarity. The people are looking to these groups for alignment, clarity, support, and decisional authority. Regardless of how flat an organization decides to function, people look to others to provide guidance on how they are expected to work.

A quick internet search on project management roles will return any number of descriptions. The same can be said about the expectations that an organization has of its employees. We've discussed here differences across organizations and highlighted examples where governance can enable as well as stall progress at an organization.

Strong governance is not just a bureaucratic function—it's the connective tissue that ensures clarity, accountability, and strategic alignment across complex research organizations. When governance is intentional, inclusive, and consistently applied, it transforms from a bottleneck into an enabler of innovation. By defining decision rights, clarifying roles, and establishing feedback mechanisms, organizations can create an operational environment where teams are empowered, projects are prioritized effectively, and resources are deployed wisely. As we transition to the next pillar, we'll explore how this foundational clarity sets the stage for building efficient, responsive project management systems that sustain innovation over time.

With governance supporting execution, we now turn to how data and insights empower smarter decisions and innovation across biopharma organizations.

Chapter 5 Takeaways

- Governance enables action when designed with purpose.
- Clear roles and responsibilities reduce bottlenecks.
- Effective governance structures evolve with the organization.
- Change starts small, leading with curiosity and questioning.
- A balance of structure and flexibility supports innovation.
- Transparency and accountability must be explicit.
- Teams thrive when governance makes their lives easier, not harder.
- Part of a committee? Practice what you preach.

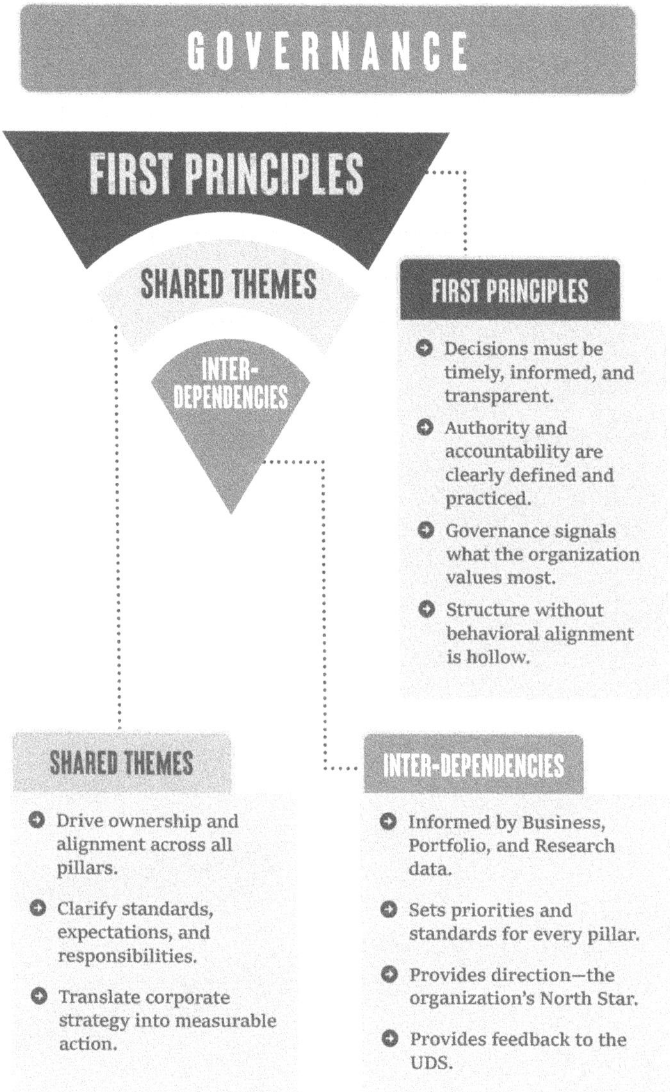

The Governance Nexus Wedge its first principles, shared themes, and interdependencies to the Biopharma Nexus.

CHAPTER 6

UNIFIED DATA STRUCTURE–THE ROOT SYSTEM AND BLUEPRINT OF OPERATIONS

INTRODUCTION: WHY EVERYTHING STARTS HERE

WALK INTO ANY high-growth biopharma company and you'll find world-class scientists, promising assets, and investment dollars flowing through. But if you peel back the curtain, what you often uncover is chaos: unclear reporting, conflicting project definitions, redundant work, and massive time drains spent reconciling data across functions.

It's not a personnel issue. It's not a technology failure. It's an architecture structure problem, rooted in the absence of a **Unified Data Structure (UDS)**. In this chapter, we lay the foundation for operational excellence by exploring why UDS matters, what it looks like in practice, and how you can begin creating it today.

You can't innovate in science without defining how you operate.

Defining Unified Data Structure

This term can be confusing and, at first glance, might appear complex. In fact, you might even be tempted to go to the next chapter. But trust me. Without getting a UDS in place, you'll only continue to experience many of the problems holding your biopharma organization back from streamlined, scalable operations.

So, what do I mean by a Unified Data Structure? At its core, UDS unifies metadata cross-functionally, enabling system-to-system traceability. Too many organizations suffer from data that's stored in various places with different names, folder structures, and ownership. Data points that might be referencing the exact same thing—but are called varying names by people from different departments—creates overwork, confusion, and a lot of employee time spent looking for certain data pieces.

Becoming a scientist at any level requires you to have rigor, through failed experimentation and a certain data discipline—accuracy, consistency, and completeness. Without those attributes in place, the experimentation conducted comes into question, and traceability becomes impossible, which increases risks, and lowers and dilutes the trust in the data intended to drive insights. The complexity within biopharma or other complex organizations is such that it necessitates budgeting, scenario planning, cross-functional updates, and demands that the data structure be mapped and consistent throughout the chosen systems of the organization.

The ability to gain insights into a data-driven decision-making organization requires the unification of data across the organization. From identifying bottlenecks to providing data context, a UDS increases visibility and traceability for the organization.

Developing the right data structure requires carefully considering the setup of your team or organization. I've outlined a few theories and frameworks that can help you think through how your data should be organized to reduce risk and optimize operations.

1. *Lean* is a framework with its foundations focused on eliminating *muda* (waste), establishing flow and standardization. Lean, just as the name states, looks to answer, "what are the fewest things that can be done that yield the greatest output?" And then, "how can we accomplish that with as little waste as possible?"

Waste for the UDS can manifest as redundant presentations, slightly modified for (sometimes similar) stakeholder groups, and long spans of time searching for pre-existing data. Inconsistent data naming presents a case of overprocessing, driving manual cross-functional translation. Where's the benefit of manually retrofitting the data from one department into another dataset for context, often misaligned in the resolution of the data? One chart is presented in quarters and another in days, for example.

2. *Six Sigma* and its principles enable consistency and reproducibility through reduction of defects. Six Sigma, named for its distance away from the process average, is often a major component of quality systems. You may not have conducted a million projects or experiments to show the two-to-three expected defects in a six-sigma system. However, errors and silos in linking systems without standard metadata reduce the data quality and will impact the pace and quality of data-driven decision-making by leadership.

3. *Systems Thinking* is perhaps a by-product of my father who served as an engineer and team lead at NASA for 40 years. Perhaps it was my internal recognition that my work contribution, however small, however siloed, was impactful to the organization and that all of our work products are related, if focused. This approach to problem-solving and decision-making focuses on the interconnectedness and interdependencies of different parts of the system.

Your organization is a system—its people, processes, and technology. All are parts of that system. As holistic parts of the system, these elements interact and influence one another, even when there are silos. When your data is not unified, you experience departments with their own language, team meetings that conclude with, "I'm not sure what they do," which leads to misaligned and delayed feedback—usually the result of poor handoffs somewhere in the reporting process.

4. *Information Architecture* is science and creativity in one. Ask yourself, how are you organizing the information or data that your company produces? It has been my experience that this knowledge

often is not captured. Sometimes the question is never even asked. What we do find are Org Charts—a tool primarily used to show functional teams and how they are organized.

Proper framework specifically looks at how you connect the various spaces, groups, and data within your organization, ensuring that they are usable and searchable. When we look at biopharma metadata specifically, we can quickly recognize some form of "Project ID," "Function," and "Phase" as common fields. These fields and others are necessary to create structure across systems. Develop the architecture fit for your company so that context remains with the data output.

5. *Sociotechnical Systems Theory* came to me mostly from experience. I didn't quite have the word for what I experienced. It was not uncommon to enter a new role at a new organization and see that there was a gross disparagement of technical skills across many systems. People within the same function had varying skill levels in the software or the tools that their function was responsible for using. It was also apparent to me that the way people worked or how their workflow was designed did not take into account how their systems were utilized.

Sociotechnical systems theory refers to the interrelatedness of social and technical aspects of an organization as a whole. For an organization to perform optimally, both the social and technical elements are required, and must be considered. In any change, any growth, any system, a major component of success is how well you bring along the stakeholders as a part of the solution. Your perspective will grow beyond the capabilities of the technical aspects of the system and will consider the social: the skills, attitudes, motivations, and values of the people and the relationships that are part of the system.

Looking back at what influenced this mindset, it's scientific training at its best. Aligning your data, ensuring its reproducibility, and presenting it in a way that answers expected questions. The Lean Six Sigma Blackbelt that evolved from one of my graduate courses provided the introduction and guidance I needed to dissect and break down complex workflows, allowing for a more structured analysis. One can't forget a favorite read of mine, *A More Beautiful Question* by Warren Berger. His writings changed my perspective on questioning, and pushed me to develop my skill in framing the Biopharma Nexus Model through great questioning.

The Power (and Pain) of Data in Biopharma

Data Is the Language of Progress

Your organization's ability to make decisions, share progress, and align teams all boils down to one question: **Can your data speak the same language across functions?**

Different departments view the world through different lenses. Research focuses on assays, compounds, and the scientifically possible. Business Operations cares about budgets, timelines, available resources, and ROI. Clinical wants enrollment metrics. CMC needs to know how much to make, under what storage conditions, for gathering estimates from vendors. But without a shared data architecture, each team starts building their own dialect, creating silos and confusion.

Let's play out those aspects for a clinical trial team working through start-up.

CMC: "We're looking to line up our distributors. Do we know how many sites we need to support? What about the countries?

ClinOps: "We have what we think will be half of our sites in the U.S. and all of our sites in Canada. We are waiting to hear back from leadership on which other countries."

Regulatory: "Can we be a part of that conversation? We need to understand where the submissions will potentially go so that we can resource adequately."

ClinOps: "Once we get input from the leadership team, we can distribute that information. We don't have a timeline on that."

Legal: "Have we selected any new sites? All we have pending is the Belgian hospital-Cliniques universitaires Saint-Luc."

CMC: "Did we already get Belgium approvals? Who is the investigator there that we are engaging with? Do they have a site number?"

Regulatory: "We just found out last week we are going into Belgium. I'm planning to submit it to authorities tomorrow."

ClinOps: "So, yes. We are going into Belgium with Dr. Vesalius. Their site number is 0701. You can get more information on Dr. Vesalius from the Medical Affairs team."

Med Affairs: "We just met them. They are a connection of our CEO."

ClinOps: "When do we think we'll have contracts and budgets ready?"

Legal: "When the budget is finalized, we can sign."

Finance: "When the contract is finalized, we can finalize the budget."

This example illustrates the collective knowledge that sits in silos, pushing a circular conversation on standard information being held by each function. Differences in language, requirements, subject matter, to name a few. All to establish a clinical site ready for enrolling patients.

At some point, you may have felt like your colleagues were from another planet. You're on the same project, but you might as well be speaking different languages. Integrating your data and using a shared language will enable alignment and speed.

The Costs of Fragmentation

You might not see it at first, but the cracks show up quickly:

- Leadership meetings are inconclusive because teams present conflicting data.

  The research team is presenting their data and their plans moving forward over the next six months. However, project management's timeline to milestones does not match up with research expectations. This disconnect lowers team credibility and leadership confidence in the progress of the project, delaying more decisions, and slowing the pace of work.

- Slide decks take weeks to prepare because the source of truth is unclear, prompting follow-up meetings.

  Cross-functional discrepancies in spend, timeline, strategies, and tasks for a given project can push a cycle of follow-ups to prepare for a leadership meeting. Your functional lead leaves the team meeting and obtains a new recommended strategy from their manager, only it was not discussed with the remainder of the team. An *adhoc* request was made to provide slides for a new potential partnership, but there isn't agreement on the strategy because other voices have contributed since then. What becomes the truth?

- Budget season becomes a full-time job of translation, reconciliation, and re-forecasting after continued leadership intervention.

  I bet you didn't think the next year's budget forecast would start the summer before. You spend four weeks reviewing what might happen in the next six months and what could happen in the next 12. Many are hypotheticals with key strategy shifts sprinkled throughout. You budget external work without any quotes, because what company would give you a quote for work nine months away? After you develop the budget, then it has to go through Finance for their stamp of approval, two operations committee reviews, and an executive leadership review. A lot of effort for not much more than educated guesses.

- Cross-functional projects stall as each team uses incompatible metadata, IDs, or terminology.

  Consider that every function in a cross-functional project has its own way of doing its work. Their systems, and their processes, all can be different. Some use presentation slides, others use spreadsheets or function-specific software. Projects move forward when everyone on board knows where the pieces are and what needs to happen next. Function-specific software, like vaults for legal documents or laboratory information management system (LIMS) for research, are typically not developed to support collaborations. The LIMS has line-by-line identifiers for each sample of an experiment. The identifiers are related only to the samples and not tied to any project. Perhaps there is a key, however, adding a layer of translation. This slows potential insights.

When your data structure is fragmented, it doesn't matter how talented your team is. Their energy gets wasted translating, reformatting, and clarifying, rather than progressing the science.

Signs You Have a Unified Data Problem

Organizations often don't realize they have a data problem because they've normalized the dysfunction. Here's how to tell:

Common Red Flags

- Each team presents data in different formats or definitions to leadership.
- Decision-making stalls because leadership "needs more data."
- Slide decks are rebuilt weekly due to inconsistent naming conventions and disjointed narratives.
- Teams inherit projects with zero context or conflicting data trails.
- You can't tell which document is the source of truth in a system that surfaces into view anything new to the platform.
- Mergers or acquisitions result in dual systems that don't talk to each other.
- Researchers waste time hunting through poorly named folders for relevant data.

The Human Toll

Beyond inefficiency, the lack of a UDS indirectly drains morale. People are frustrated. High performers leave. Collaboration becomes turf warfare.

In 2025, a scientific data and AI cloud company in Boston estimated north of 10 million data silos created across biopharma. Described as a "nasty maze of silos," they appeared at the company level, between geographically dispersed locations, at the department level, and at the lab level. An online R&D-focused news site described the gap of raw, unstructured data as not being of use to artificial intelligence. As the changing times point to deeper integration of existing data with artificial intelligence, companies are encouraged to focus on data engineering and its harmonization, and to develop a standard schema.[17]

To address the lack of alignment reported, language was harmonized, and an AI cloud was integrated, reaching out to silos. As a by-product of these improvements, the morale of customers was found to have improved following the eight-month cloning selection process, being brought down to two months, as data was now available in a single place, not multiple silos.

Another company in the same space points to lack of standardization, manual data errors, and lack of quality control as contributing to the need to repeat experiments and clinical trials. The risk is high, especially in complex, regulated industries. These issues can extend far beyond any immediate financial loss. With an estimated $90 billion flowing annually into R&D, having a Unified Data Structure is essential to survival for any biopharma.[18]

---

17 Brian Buntz, "TerraScience's Strategy for Liberating Biopharma Data from an 10 Million Silos," *R&D World*, May 5, 2025, https://www.rdworldonline.com/tetrasciences-strategy-for-liberating-biopharma-data-from-an-estimated-10-million-silos.

18 "Data Mine to Data Minefield: The Hidden Costs of Poor Data Quality in Biopharma R&D," *Elucidata* (blog), January 15, 2025, https://www.elucidata.io/blog/data-mine-to-data-minefield-the-hidden-costs-of-poor-data-quality-in-biopharma-r-d.

The human toll of these challenges was explored through a recent scoping article, a review that explored available literature on causes, consequences, and strategies to deal with information overload. When we create silos, and our data is disconnected, our teams are up against multiple sources with multiple entry points, adding to an overload of information. This overload can lead to confusion and difficulty in processing information effectively, leading to poor decision-making and a feeling of stress, adding to slow processing.

A total of 89 papers met eligibility criteria to be included in the review out of an initial collection of more than 11,000 found through database searches. Shahrzadi et al. uncovered the most effective causes and contributing factors to information overload.[19] In addition to the typical complexity of information (a common feature of complex industries) was an overabundance of irrelevant, contradictory, and incorrect information effectively polluting the information pool. Further, even setting aside an individual's characteristics, which can vary greatly in their ability to process complex data, the authors pointed to characteristics of the information itself, such as an increase in quantity of the number and variety of sources.

Certainly, the causes and contributing factors must be understood, but Shahrzadi's review highlighted critical consequences of information overload, especially their impact on operations. Making the list was low work efficiency and productivity of individuals and their organizations, as well as poor decision-making due to limited information quality and effectiveness.

---

19 Leila Shahrzadi et al., "Causes, Consequences, and Strategies to Deal with Information Overload: A Scoping Review," *International Journal of Information Management Data Insights* 4, no. 2 (2024): 100261, https://doi.org/10.1016/j.jjimei.2024.100261.

Those findings are in line with information challenges we experience every day. They highlight the apprehension we all have when venturing into a company server or folder structure: What's new? What's accurate? What's still being developed? Unfortunately, organizations fail to recognize the toll on workers and their productivity caused by the effect of combing through toxic landfills of sloppy data or half-baked information.

Why Those Effects Happen—And Why They're Not Your Fault

Most organizations don't set out to create a fragmented data ecosystem. But it evolves that way. And when you aren't expecting it, it eventually turns into the ball of Christmas lights sitting in your attic.

Early-Stage Survival Mode

Consider an early-stage, recently funded biopharma company with a promising new AI/Oncology spin. They've just been awarded a joint $200 million runway to fund the next three years to produce their first prototype. Hypothetically, let's call them AI Biosciences. The North Star for this endeavor is a prototype, focusing the efforts on talent, science, and speed.

What they don't have is time to wait until everyone is hired to begin work on the program. To respond, the company speeds up their hiring to get scientists into chairs and working on the deliverable, a prototype three years away.

They focused first on the talent that would push the first year's work full throttle. Then, a year later, they hired the remainder, and hired added support a year after that. To their dismay, each newly hired group created their own systems to manage their specific functions, not to necessarily connect them to others.

At the start, the focus is on science and speed. You get a funding cost of anywhere from six to nine figures to hire teams, run experiments, and chase milestones. Data management and structure is an afterthought, handled through whatever tools are easiest for the team at the moment.

Each department begins creating its own naming conventions, folder structures, and reporting systems. Without shared standards, everyone optimizes for their own reality, from their own unique experiences, and the problems compound over time.

We already saw Massachusetts biopharma companies alone raised nearly $8 billion in 2024. That's a lot of teams scaling quickly to win the rat race. Existing data, vision, and market potential are the main targets for funding allocation. Rarely is the target how well an organization is structured or the policies that they integrate.

Growth Without Coordination

The new funding that prompted new hires now requires decision-makers as the company expects expansion. Naturally with growth, the tendency is for more and more bureaucratic layers. Teams specialize. New vendor software becomes available. Systems proliferate. Eventually, leadership realizes that they need "alignment," but by then, the data foundation is already cracked. Who is going to own the change?

Every time you rename something slightly differently—project versus initiative, compound versus candidate—you create a fork in your data. Do it a few dozen times, and you've built a monster.

How to Begin Fixing It

The good news? You don't need to overhaul everything overnight. You do, though, need to **start somewhere**.

Step 1: Ask the Right Questions

To identify what data matters, begin by asking what is critical to delivering on the strategy.

- Are we selecting the right projects?
- Do the projects have the right partners?
- Are teams adequately resourced to execute what is required for success?
- What does success look like for us?

Resources have limitations, especially in biopharma. Planning for capacity, we can ask ourselves

- How much does a project cost us?
- What is our projected ROI per phase?
- Are projects adequately resourced?

- How much of the budget has been consumed?
- What are the current workloads by department?
- Who is responsible for doing what, and by when?
- How are all the activities connected to delivering on the corporate strategy?

Each question requires consistent metadata across systems, namely

- Project Name
- Phase
- Department
- Function
- Expense Category
- Owner
- Domain

STEP 2: BUILD CONSENSUS AROUND LANGUAGE

Your teams already know how to work, but they likely describe the same thing differently. Bring in four to five key cross-functional players and conduct a **nomenclature and glossary workshop** to answer

- What does "project" mean in R&D vs. Portfolio Operations?
- What does "site" mean to Legal vs. CMC vs. Clinical?
- How do we structure and maintain data synchronicity as assets move through development?

- What's the minimum metadata we need to make sense of those answers?

UDS Nomenclature in Action: Clinical Chaos

A clinical-stage company had over 150 employees and several Phase III trials. But project updates were painful. Legal referenced hospital names. CMC used internal site codes. Project managers named the investigator.

The solution? We created a concatenated data tag that included all three—legal name, internal code, and investigator—so that every department spoke the same language. This simple adjustment was adopted globally and enabled quick insights that previously took hours to generate.

Step 3: Structure Your Stack Intentionally

Don't let your tech stack grow accidentally. For every system you add, ask

- Can it connect to our other tools?
- Can we report from it?
- Does it align with our shared nomenclature?
- Who owns the data it produces?
- Who will be the internal process owner with all the responsibilities?
- How can it connect to key stakeholders?

Step 4: Train Like You Mean It

UDS is worthless if no one knows how to use it. You must document, train, and empower, not just hope tribal knowledge will carry over.

"Bob told Sarah, who told Josh, etc, and now no one's trained properly." That's how bad habits become company culture.

UDS in Action—From Dysfunction to Clarity

Imagine this:

- A project manager builds a slide deck in an hour instead of a week.
- A new employee finds every experiment tied to a project, instantly.
- Leadership asks for direction, and the right data appears, automatically.

These aren't dreams. They're what happens when a company invests in UDS.

UDS in Action with Company Change: R&D Merger Mayhem

One R&D organization acquired another and couldn't explain their portfolio status. They used three systems with mismatched hierarchies: one went Program → Project → Goals → Activities, while the other used Program → Product → Project → Goals → Sprints.

Each mismatch created "translation points" where data had to be manually interpreted. That resulted in wasted time, missed insights, and zero transparency.

They didn't need new tools. They needed alignment.

Culture and Buy-In—Why It Must Be Everyone's Job

UDS is not an IT problem. It's not a portfolio manager's problem. It's an **organizational mandate**.

How to Get Buy-In

1. **Lead with the pain**: Show teams how much time they're wasting today.
2. **Speak with empathy**: Empathy opens much larger conversations and can reveal unspoken truths.
3. **Start small**: Don't boil the ocean. Align one workflow or team at a time connected to the bigger picture.
4. **Stay connected to the people doing the work**: They know where the pain lives. They'll be the ones to carry the solution forward.
5. **Show wins early**: Communicate before and after to a wider audience to show real change and real action.
6. **Celebrate simplification**: You don't need fancy features. You need clarity.

You have rules no one wrote, systems no one owns, and chaos that was somehow missed during your interview. You can change that disorder. You just need a map. The Biopharma Nexus is that map.

What You Gain When You Get It Right

UDS isn't just about cleaning up your digital closet. It's about unlocking performance.

Tangible Outcomes

- faster, more confident decision-making
- higher employee morale and retention
- sharper insights into resource allocation and ROI
- easier onboarding for new hires and functions
- smarter system integration and vendor management

The more successful you are at maintaining a unified approach to your data, the more your growing pains feel like hiccups, not emergencies.

UNIFIED DATA STRUCTURE LESSONS IN ACTION

Case Study 1: Oncology Therapeutics—Building a Common Language from Chaos

When I stepped into my role as a program manager with Oncology, the company was gearing up for its first-ever Phase III clinical trial. We were launching in 17 countries, across 175 sites, and from the jump, I could tell we were speaking completely different languages internally. Not metaphorically—literally.

The clinical ops team would reference investigators: "Dr. Smith," "Dr. Nasir." Legal spoke in terms of the hospital's legal entity, which rarely matched what the clinical team used. Finance, on the other hand, relied on site numbers that corresponded to regions or countries—site 001 might be Boston, site 300 could be in Belgium. And not one of these systems talked to each other, creating data fragments that required manual manipulation to align.

During team meetings, we'd spend the first 10 minutes trying to figure out who we were even talking about. "Which site is that again?" "Is that Dr. Nasir?" "Institute Gustave Roussy?" "Oh, wait, are we talking about 207 or 309?" It was like translating across three dialects, all in real time. This lack of alignment wasn't just frustrating. It was risky. We were spending millions launching sites and had no consistent naming convention to track progress.

The breakthrough came when I proposed a unified nomenclature system to key stakeholders: a concatenated ID that included the site number, the hospital/legal entity, and the lead investigator's name. It gave every team a common anchor. Legal could still search by contract, clinical by doctor, and finance by site ID, but now we could cross-reference all three seamlessly, bringing power to our analyses.

We embedded this structure into our system workflows, allowing us to create real-time dashboards with meaningful insight. Instead of having a hundred scattered spreadsheets and project trackers, we had one unified system. It wasn't perfect, but it worked.

The impact was immediate. Contract status updates no longer required a 30-minute scavenger hunt. We could pull reports by country, by investigator, or by trial phase. We saw where the delays were happening and why. We were finally making decisions based on a full picture—not just the fragment someone happened to bring to the meeting. Above all, we had data. Real data from our own trial that provided new baselines to compete against, rather than arbitrary expectations from the internet.

The Unified Data Structure didn't just help us get through that trial. It changed how we operated across clinical, legal, and finance teams. It was the first time I saw the real power of alignment—and how clarity in data structure can drive clarity in decision-making.

Case Study 2: Discovery Therapeutics—From Project Chaos to Portfolio Control

When Discovery Therapeutics brought me on to consult, they didn't ask for help fixing data systems. They wanted a project manager for a mid-stage R&D program, the latest in their pipeline. But it didn't take long before I saw the bigger problem: Each team had built its own version of "the truth."

Timelines were kept in static slide decks, formatted however the team lead preferred, updated whenever they were needed for a leadership call. Milestones varied in how they were named, ordered, or categorized. Actions, decisions, and risks were stored in online documents scattered across a filing system—or just lived in someone's memory. If you wanted to know what was happening across programs, you had to go on a digital scavenger hunt.

Worse, each project had its own tool preferences. One team used spreadsheets connected to the cloud, while others used spreadsheet software that remained on their local computer. Neither had everything they needed. A third used document software to recreate legacy spreadsheets. There was no way to roll it up, no consistent metadata, and no shared language.

I saw the chaos as a huge opportunity to leverage their project management software, as I had years of experience and could drive transformation.

I started small. I built a program timeline template and asked whether I could use it to manage my assigned project. I added automation for meeting follow-ups, action-item notifications, and milestone alerts. Over time, I layered in dashboards so that leadership could see real-time status at the project level. Then we added portfolio-level views.

The key wasn't just the software—it was the structure. I used the same milestones and naming conventions across programs. I defined what "in progress," "final," and "executed" actually meant. We created drop-down menus for disease areas, trial phases, and risk categories. Suddenly, data wasn't just being entered—it was being standardized.

This visibility allowed us to do something that had been impossible before: portfolio-wide reporting. We could see which programs were off-track, which functions were overloaded, and where to reallocate resources in real-time.

Eventually, the system became our governance engine. Leadership started using the dashboard to decide which teams had to present at governance reviews. If your project wasn't self-declared yellow or red, you didn't need to prepare a deck. Business as usual. This synthesis alone saved teams dozens of hours per quarter for multiple people. It improved the visibility and communication to leadership. They went from static slides to a live view, pointing leadership to key data and areas of friction, and focusing leadership support on the areas that needed it most. As the portfolio grows, so will their collective understanding of the health of their organization in any sense of the word.

I didn't come in expecting to rebuild their data infrastructure, but that's what happened. And once we had it, everything else—governance, decision-making, and strategic alignment—became exponentially easier. The organization began to scale together.

Case Study 3: Innovations Biotech—Scaling Without Structure

Innovations Biotech was an ambitious company—funded, fast-growing, and full of talent. But when I joined as an operational consultant, I quickly realized they were running with no consistent digital footprint. It was a digital Wild West.

One team used a software development platform, another used a low-code project management software. A third was experimenting with a well-known online server. Each group tracked their tasks, decisions, and progress independently—using tools and structures that made sense for them, but not for anyone else. There was no single source of truth. In fact, leadership had recently issued a mandate that "all project management must now be done in this tool!" But nobody had trained the teams on how to use it, and worse, that tool didn't fit the needs of half the departments.

The result? Mismatched timelines, duplicated effort, and an alarming number of overdue tasks that no one even knew were overdue. One PM said, "I was just told to copy the plan into the system. I'm not actually managing the project there."

We were working on complex, sequential processes (like an R&D assembly line), but each team ran its portion on a different track. Imagine passing a baton in a relay race where every runner is in a different stadium. That's what it felt like.

I tried to reframe the issue: This wasn't a software problem. It was a structure problem. So, I mapped out the full end-to-end workflow and identified the key milestones. Then, I proposed a cross-functional nomenclature for tasks and phases. Not every team needed to use the same tool, but we needed to use the same language.

Unfortunately, leadership wasn't aligned—a challenge that existed as a result of a rotating client sponsor over short periods of time. Some believed that fixing one team's process would be enough. There were cross-functional projects with no alignment on targets, requirements, process ownership, or governance. Multimillion-dollar projects were running on strategic concepts and no operations. Others thought they could scale without addressing the underlying data architecture. I was told to pause the engagement just as we were about to implement shared frameworks.

It was a missed opportunity. Without a Unified Data Structure, even the most talented teams will drown in ambiguity. And the faster you grow, the faster the cracks will show. Innovations Biotech had the resources and the brainpower. What they lacked was the connective tissue, which is what a unified data strategy really is.

Conclusion: The Root System for What Comes Next

Before you fix your portfolio, before you optimize research operations, and before you reorganize your business ops, you must build your root system.

Your UDS is not a spreadsheet or a piece of software. It is a shared mindset, a governance practice, a representation, and a way of working that ensures your company can scale while maintaining visibility on operational risk and productivity.

It's the foundation that everything else stands on in biopharma.

And without it?

You're just building beautiful plans on broken ground.

Chapter 6 Takeaways

- Dysfunction often comes from mismatched language and naming conventions.
- Problems arise gradually over time, rarely at a single point.
- UDS is not an IT problem. It's an organizational mandate.
- Early wins in alignment build momentum and construct internal bridges.
- Without UDS, your plans will be built on a broken foundation.
- UDS is as cultural as it is technical, requiring empathy, patience, and persistence.

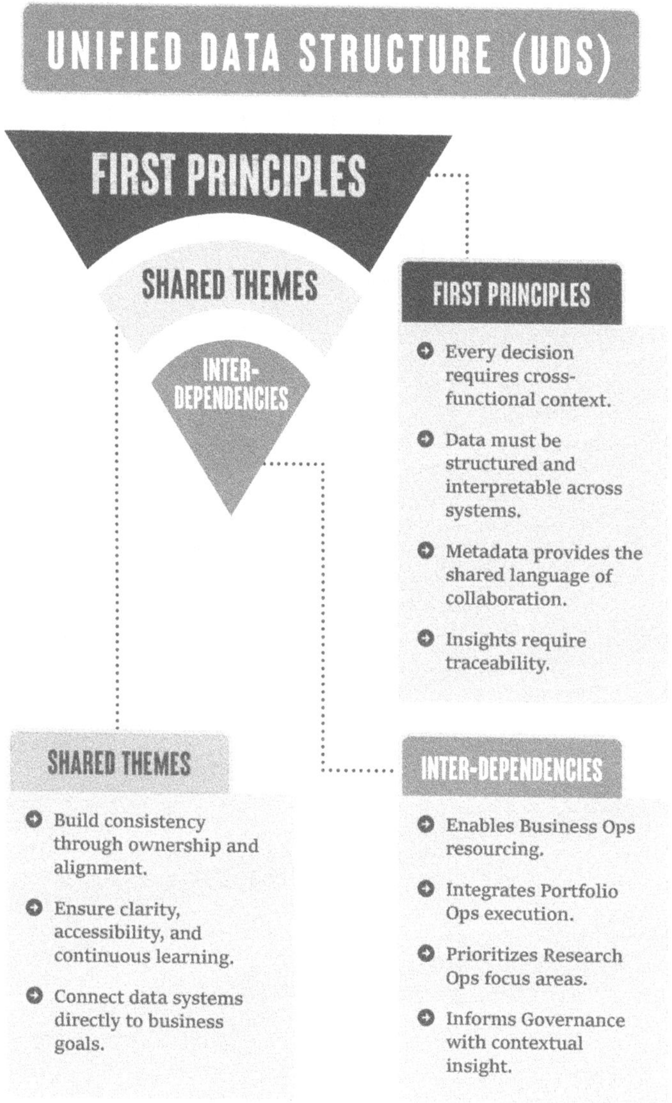

The Unified Data Structure (UDS) Nexus Wedge its first principles, shared themes, and interdependencies to the Biopharma Nexus.

EPILOGUE

MOVING FORWARD WITH OPERATIONAL EXCELLENCE

TAKE A BREATH. That's the first thing I'd tell you as we wrap up this book. If you've made it to this point, you've engaged with a lot of ideas and challenges. This isn't a lightweight subject. It's not a simple fix. We're talking about rethinking how teams function inside a biopharma organization. And we're doing it in a way that goes beyond tools and technologies. It's about changing the mindset and the culture around how we work.

Throughout my career, I've seen one consistent pattern: Companies try to boil the ocean. They want to fix everything at once. They recognize that things aren't working as smoothly as they could be—too many delays, too much friction, and too much uncertainty—and they think the answer is a massive overhaul. But that's not sustainable, and it's usually not necessary.

What I've learned, and what I want to emphasize here, is that you don't have to solve *everything*. You need to start by identifying the most *critical workflows*—the processes that carry the most weight in terms of decision-making, those that frequently break down, and those that your teams rely on but barely understand. That's where the value lies. That's where real transformation starts.

That's why we developed Biopharma Nexus Operational Risk Assessments. These assessments were the curation of over 25 years combined of experience in a complex industry like biopharma.

The assessments are designed to help teams quickly identify and prioritize the most fragile and impactful workflows in their operations. We grouped our assessments over four modules: I. Facilities Management, II. Scientific and Operational Workflow Integration, III. Execution & Governance Excellence, and IV. Support Systems & Infrastructure Integrity. Each module has its own risk factors and workflow scoring, and embodies the following dimensions: fragility (how easily they break down), visibility (how transparent they are to others), stakeholder load (how many people rely on them), and resilience (how well they adapt when disrupted). It's not about tracking everything. It's about knowing where to focus, which is understanding the risk with the biggest blast radius.

This process usually uncovers blind spots—places where people are manually tracking decisions, key activities that lack guidance, patching solutions together, or just hoping everything holds up under pressure. Those aren't small inefficiencies. They're structural weaknesses. And the more complex your science, the more those weak points matter.

One of the core themes throughout this book is that **operational excellence in Biopharma isn't just about efficiency—it's about resilience**. It's about designing systems and structures that can support innovation, absorb uncertainty, and still deliver results. It means building visibility into your processes. It means reducing dependencies on tribal knowledge. It means documenting what matters, automating what you can, and making it easier for people to focus on their work instead of constantly firefighting.

If you've made it this far, you might be wondering what your next steps should be. Here's what I recommend:

First, if you're looking for a place to start, visit sigmalabconsulting.com to learn about our Operational Risk Assessment consulting engagements. We created these assessments to help teams self-assess and debrief one-on-one with our consultants. In days, not months, you'll end up with a report designed to give you a clearer picture of where your organization is strong, where you're vulnerable, and where you should focus next. Think of it as a low-stakes way to start the conversation inside your company.

Second, if you want support, we offer full consulting services at Sigma Lab Consulting that help you walk through the same Biopharma Nexus process we use with clients. These engagements don't end with generic slide decks or reports. They're tailored engagements—partnerships where we work directly with your team to define your biggest pain points and co-create a strategy to address them, and then facilitate the execution and adoption.

Third, just reach out. If you have a question, a half-formed idea, or even a gut feeling that something's off but you can't quite put your finger on it, send a message. Sometimes, the biggest breakthroughs start with a simple conversation. You don't need a formal proposal. You just need curiosity and a willingness to look at things differently.

More than anything, I hope this book has helped you **reframe the problem**. That focus is not about forcing science into a box. It's about creating the right infrastructure so that science can thrive. It's about removing the friction that slows people down. It's about aligning the everyday operations of research teams with the broader strategic goals of the business.

That kind of alignment doesn't happen by accident. It requires intentional design. It requires people who can ask better questions, like:

- What does operational success look like in our context?
- What decisions are we still flying blind on?
- Who's making this work easier? Who's still feeling left out?
- What tools or habits are we relying on that no longer serve us?

These questions are your roadmap. You won't answer all of them overnight, but they'll point you in the right direction. Use them to guide your next steps. Use them to shape the conversations you're having with your teams. Use them to elevate the quality of your operational thinking.

Finally, don't forget that this is a journey, not a destination. You're going to uncover things you didn't know were broken. You're going to find opportunities you didn't know existed. You're going to hit some roadblocks. That's okay. What matters is that you keep moving forward—and that you do it with purpose. Eventually, others will climb on board because you make things better. You.

Thank you for reading. I hope this book has given you not just insights but a framework for action. Now, let's get to work.

ACKNOWLEDGMENTS

IF I'VE LEARNED anything over the course of my education and professional careers, it's that life has a way of humbling you. And when that happens, we should welcome the lessons with open arms. The people I surrounded myself with showed me there was more to this world.

To my teachers, instructors, and professors who have played a role in my understanding of life sciences and business. At one point, education became much less about what knowledge I learned and more about how it developed my understanding of life. Over my challenges during university coursework, I encountered some amazing professors who found a thread, looked beyond the marks in any course, and helped me bridge a new understanding and unique perspective so I could be successful. Thank you for seeing the struggle and reaching out a hand.

To my colleagues and peers who held space for me to ask questions and enabled my curiosity in their work. You created a hyperdrive for my learning and understanding of this industry, from your perspective. Thank you for your patience when I peppered you with questions after working through obstacles from a lack of understanding. You've become trusted peers and friends I feel blessed to have come across.

To my managers and mentors:

Steve—you were the first outside of family to truly make me feel seen. You saw my thirst for understanding and my internal desire to leave my mark in the sciences. As I struggled, feeling inadequate and falling short on my career aspirations early on, you saw me for what I was capable of accomplishing. You once told me, "I've never known someone to work as hard as you and not succeed." Well, here I am. And I will continue to do so. Thank you.

Ran—you took a chance on me when I was but an infant in the industry. Because of you, I received opportunities I thought were decades away. You brought me in, listened to my ideas, and helped create a powerful sense of self that I was more than any one system I was proficient in. Challenging me to own a transformation and lead it has carved my vision into what Sigma Lab Consulting is today. Thank you.

Jared—to this day I'm not exactly sure what you saw, but almost immediately, I felt a sense of trust: trust in me to develop best practices internally and to drive a project forward through communication and alignment. You trusted me as a confidant when you needed perspective. I recall stepping into a meeting with leaders, assuming I was there to capture minutes, then realizing what you wanted was my perspective on an issue that touched the organization deeply. You've helped me evolve my understanding of leadership. Thank you.

Elena—your mentorship gave Sigma Lab Consulting a real chance for success in transitioning from six-figure stable jobs into entrepreneurship. You pushed us to consider key perspectives to build a successful business. As a listener, you created a space for us to communicate our vision and provided the right mix of feedback and come-to-Jesus moments. Your listening ear and insightful questioning have pushed us to challenge our own assumptions and to become the type of business that makes a difference. Thank you.

To my parents, the foundation of my work ethic, and to my siblings. Your unwavering support gave me confidence that it would all work out, even at points in my life when I was not sure what direction to go. Thank you.

To my business partner Lawrence. Your curiosity has helped build something we can both be proud of, and you continue to challenge me, including writing this book. Cheers to you, a major contributor to the success of our first venture. Thank you.

To my wife, Michelle, my self-proclaimed biggest cheerleader and the source of a better me. I can't overstate what your support has meant to me. Your friendship, partnership, and love have grown my patience, empathy, and compassion and have helped me become the best version of myself for our family and for you. Thank you for being a listening ear and sounding board on this journey, trusting me every step of the way.

To Julie Broad and the entire Book Launchers team, from my writer, editors, and fact-checkers to my marketers, designers, and account managers for the guidance and tools to start this movement and build this book. Well done.

LET'S KEEP THE CONVERSATION GOING

See how the ideas from Predictably Broken work in a real world application by exploring our suite of Operational Risk Assessments at:
sigmalabconsulting.com/assessments

Sign up for email updates and behind-the-scenes insights for building smarter operations at:
sigmalabconsulting.com/predictablybroken

Tune in to the **Lean by Design podcast** at your favorite podcast platform.

CONNECT WITH OSCAR AT...

Instagram: @sciguy_insights

Linkedin: oagonzalez07

Linktree: sigmalabconsulting

THANK YOU FOR READING!

If you enjoyed *Predictably Broken*, please leave a review on Goodreads or on the retailer site where you purchased this book.

www.ingramcontent.com/pod-product-compliance
Ingram Content Group UK Ltd.
Pitfield, Milton Keynes, MK11 3LW, UK
UKHW020123290926
15471UKWH00003B/246